# AN ELABORATE GESTURE
# OF PASTNESS
## Three Films by Dani Gal

*Night and Fog*
*As from Afar*
*White City*

# FOREWORD

In 2019 Jade Niklai invited me to Vienna for a residency at Blood Mountain Projects to develop a new work and to comprehensively showcase my practice. During the residency, Jade also connected me with the Vienna Wiesenthal Institute for Holocaust Studies where I became a research fellow. In this environment I started to map the web of connections and references that has transformed into this publication. The foundations of this book were created through the process of sorting images and texts that I had collected during the production of the film trilogy titled *An Elaborate Gesture of Pastness*.

During my time in Vienna, I met Noit Banai. Our long conversations about my films resulted in the opening essay in this book. The essay addresses hallucinatory cinema, which in the words of Noit, "raise questions about its own role as an instrument for the production and reproduction of the effects and affects of the real". Noit was introduced to me by Sabeth Buchmann, who has been involved in this project from its early stages. Sabeth and I engaged in a series of extended conversations between August and December 2020 that revolve around ethical, moral, historical and aesthetic dilemmas. During this period, the debate in Germany around anti-Semitism, Holocaust remembrance, decolonialism and Israel–Palestine rose to unforeseeably controversial levels and became an unavoidable backdrop to our conversation. The third position in the book started to develop a year ago when Burcu Dogramaci approached me for an interview. In turn, I asked her to extend this conversation into a reflection on the trilogy. In her essay, Burcu writes about the migranti-sation of history and society as a call to examine fixed notions of history. The last text in the book is by Sa'ed Atshan, whom I met in 2018 during his research trip to Berlin. I decided to invite Sa'ed to reflect primarily on my film *White City*, and he writes, "I confront the issues not just as a schol-ar and anthropologist, but also as a Palestinian", concluding my book with a personal but nevertheless political tone.

I am grateful to Michael Rothberg for his support and scholarship, which functions as one of the umbrella concepts for this book. Special thanks goes to Jade Niklai for producing this publication, to Mika Hayashi Ebbesen for the editorial input, to Olga Prader for the layout design and to Alexis Zavialoff for publishing it. I would also like to thank all those involved in the making of my film trilogy, namely the producers Jonathan Dowek and Caroline Kirberg and the directors of photography Emre Erkmen and Itay Marom.

Lastly, I would like to thank the authors who, through their conver-sant and insightful contributions, contextualise my films within the fields of memory politics, film studies, Holocaust and postcolonial studies and historiography. Furthermore, these scholars' personal experiences and positions, as descendants of historical victims, perpetrators, refugees and migrants, mirror the themes discussed in this book and enable the publi-cation to become a vigorous platform for discussing the present and the future through the past.

Dani Gal
Berlin, February 2021

The myths and concepts of the past, I would emphasize, help us to see the present not because they are being re-lived in an "eternal present", but because they acquire new significances and altered meanings in a simulacrum of what has already passed. It is only by puncturing the counterfeit of similitude that the reality of dissimilitude becomes visible.

Rustom Bharucha, *Terror and Performance*, Routledge, New York, 2014, p. 13.

Bei Nacht und Nebel

Bei Nacht und Nebel fahr' ich fort,
Frag' nicht, wohin es geht?
Denn ach, was Liebes ließ ich dort,
Das noch am Fenster steht.
Vom lieben Mund das Abschiedswort
Ich hör' es früh und spät.
Das treue Aug' bleibt immerfort
Der Stern, der mit mir geht.

Night and Fog

At night and in the fog, I depart;
Do not ask whither!
For ah, what dear [person] did I leave behind
Who is still standing at the window!
The parting word from her dear lips
I hear it early and late.
Her faithful eye remains always
The star that travels with me

Christian Reinhold Köstlin (1813–1856), English translation by Sharon Krebs.

Dani Gal, *Night and Fog*, 2011, film still, camera: Itay Marom

# HALLUCINATORY CINEMA AND THE DIALOGICAL POLITICS OF FRAMING
Noit Banai

## INTRODUCTION:
## SCREEN, STORYTELLING
## AND HUMAN SENSORIUM

There is something unnerving about Dani Gal's trilogy and its simultaneous emergence from and constitution of the folds, textures and intersections of history and memory. In films that re-enact events whose potency continues to shape our collective imaginary, Gal has developed a *hallucinatory cinema* that raises questions about its own role as an instrument for the production and reproduction of the effects and affects of the real. This cinema, working through an idiom of realism and the medium's own techniques, conventions and histories, transforms the complex zones of indeterminacy between fact and fiction into an unsettling corporal and visual experience. To shape this dreamlike territory between the real and its representations, Gal taps into a vast conscious and unconscious archive of still and moving images through which historical events and their aftermaths have been mediated and diffused to diverse publics. There is Alain Resnais's *Nuit et brouillard* (*Night and Fog*, 1956), Liliana Cavani's *Il portiere di notte* (*The Night Porter*, 1974), and Elia Suleiman's *Chronicles of a Disappearance* (1996), just to name a few. It is through these films and many others that the history of the Holocaust, the relationship between Jewish survivors and German perpetrators, and the experience of Palestinian statelessness in the wake of Al Nakba have been given a visual language.[1]

While each of Gal's films, *White City* (2018), *As from Afar* (2013) and *Night and Fog* (2011) fluently speaks the language of cinematic realism and its historical precedents, it also becomes clear that the syntax is different. Scenes have all the trappings of verisimilitude: actors often recite lines taken directly from historical documents, while objects and materials refer to specific times and places and appear historically authentic. At the same time, Gal's cinematography — a careful manipulation of scale, framing, narrative and sound — means that our sense of temporality and point of view are recurrently jumbled, and the visual and auditory immersion required to preserve a semblance of the real is frequently disrupted. Together, these elements and techniques overwhelmingly work together to sustain a "reality effect" while simultaneously breaking with naturalistic conventions in ways that make visible the phantasmic qualities of reality.[2] In this strange cohabitation of referential plenitude and disorientation, the films buzz with connotations and juxtapositions that generate a polyphonic relation to the world. As "everything signifies ceaselessly and several times", mimetic realism's claims to a single, unshakeable truth are questioned and the malleability of representation comes to the fore.[3]

Yet, Gal goes much farther: By amplifying the links to the exterior, he opens up a multi-voiced hallucinatory zone that is produced cinematically yet goes beyond the realm of cinema. Wending its way between screen effects, storyline and human sensorium, hallucinatory cinema circulates within individual, collective and national bodies; it also blends and chafes histories and memories that have largely remained secure within discrete national archives and organised around fixed hierarchies of power; and it fundamentally interrogates the way in which various modern nation states, as biopolitical nervous systems, have invented mecha-

---

1    According to Haim Bresheeth, "[...] the Nakba in Palestinian or Arab films was noticeable by its absence. This is far from surprising; the images of loss and destruction meted out by the Zionist forces to the many hundreds of thousands of Palestinian refugees are far from easy for Arabs, especially for Palestinians to confront. A long time had to pass until the Nakba could become a live topic within Palestinian cultural life, serving both the need to purge the trauma as well as to construct identity. A whole generation of Palestinians had to grow up without hardly any cinematic representations of the great catastrophe of 1948 as well as the acts of resistance that were part of their history. This reminds us of a similar attitude (though for different reasons) in Israel toward the Holocaust in the 1950s. The images of Jews led to the slaughter were an abomination for the Zionists of post-World War II Palestine — the old Jew of Europe has always been seen as an embarrassment for Zionism, a motivating negativity that propelled it to construct the *New Jew*, the Israeli Zionist. Thus, visual representations of the Holocaust, and especially cinematic representations were very rare in this formative period in Israel". See "The Continuity of Trauma and Struggle: Recent Cinematic Representations of the Nakba", in *Nakba: Palestine, 1948, and the Claims of Memory*, ed. Ahmad H. Sa'di and Lila Abu-Lughod, Columbia University Press, New York, 2007, p. 163–64.
2    Roland Barthes, "The Reality Effect", *The Rustle of Language*, trans. Richard Howard, University of California Press, Berkeley, 1989.
3    Roland Barthes, *S/Z*, trans. Richard Miller, Hill and Wang, New York, 1974, p. 11–12.

nisms for the production of racialised otherness.[4] To turn categories of knowledge upside down and back to front, rearrange the borders of the known and awaken new possibilities via visual and corporal experiences is a tricky but urgent undertaking. Today, as nation states in both liberal and illiberal democracies continue to formulate novel forms of racism, and the entanglements between modernity and coloniality become more articulated in the public sphere, it is vital to ask how the negotiations of history and memory through a hallucinatory cinema might connect to the political stakes of the present.

## THE POLITICS OF FRAMING

The trilogy is constructed around three encounters between protagonists who have been seminal to the construction of twentieth-century German, Jewish and Arab histories. In *White City*, we accompany Arthur Ruppin, Zionist leader in charge of the Jewish settlement of Palestine, as he seeks out Hans F. K. Günther, German eugenicist of the Weimar Republic and Third Reich, and finds inspiration in the Weißenhofsiedlung (Weissenhof Estate) in Stuttgart; in *As from Afar*, we are privy to conversations between Simon Wiesenthal, Holocaust survivor and Nazi hunter, and Albert Speer, chief Nazi architect and Minister for Armaments and War Production; and in *Night and Fog*, we are beside Michael Goldman-Gilad, investigative officer for the Adolf Eichmann trial, during the cremation and scattering of Eichmann's ashes at sea.[5] These curious historical collisions become the basis for what historian Michael Rothberg has called "multidirectional memory". This model moves away from the premise that collective memory is a "scarce resource" or a "zero-sum struggle for preeminence" and instead calls for a dialogical, intercultural approach that is "subject to ongoing negotiation, cross-referencing, and borrowing".[6] With this shift, diverse traditions of genocide and colonialism can be thought of together in their historical relatedness while simultaneously "working through the partial overlaps and conflicting claims that constitute the archives of memory and the terrain of politics".[7] Stated another way, multidirectional memory — with its mobility and metamorphosis via interlacing

4    Michael Taussig, *The Nervous System*, Routledge, London, 1992.
5    Adolf Eichmann's trial began before a special tribunal of the Jerusalem District Court on 11 April 1961; he was indicted on and eventually convicted of fifteen criminal charges, including crimes against humanity, war crimes, crimes against the Jewish people and membership in a criminal organisation; he was found guilty and executed by hanging on 1 June 1962.
6    Michael Rothberg, *Multidirectional Memory: Remembering the Holocaust in the Age of Decolonization*, Stanford University Press, Stanford, 2009, p. 3; Mikhail Bakhtin has offered the most sustained concept of the dialogic in *The Dialogic Imagination: Four Essays*, ed. Michael Holquist, trans. Carl Emerson and Michael Holquist, University of Texas Press, Austin, 1981.
7    Rothberg, *Multidirectional Memory*, p. 29.

The forms and consequences of the empathic unsettlement required to address traumatic events cannot
be predictable or known. Its role is precisely this — to
disrupt. It emanates from a fear of any type of closure,
to which all political discourse aspires and which itself
is a harbinger of fascist logic.

Disruption is the key word here, since it is located
between the two poles that trauma is liable to generate:
disruption neither completely dismantles the discourse
(as a field of distinctions), nor does it fortify dichotomous
opposition. It introduces some rather indigestible
otherness to the discursive sphere, which emanates
from an ethical commitment to those experiencing the
trauma, but that cannot necessarily be formulated
immediately. As such, empathic unsettlement disrupts
and constantly undermines every "redeeming narrative"
of suffering that offers a melancholic pleasure, and
this is the source of its considerable political value.
One might say that it compels us to take the otherness
of the other seriously. It operates in the twilight zone
between full identification, which appropriates the other
or requires her to submit to the concepts of the "self,"
and outright alienation, which generates a sphere from
which communication is absent, in which only power
dictates. The weakened identification experienced as part
of empathic unsettlement is therefore sensed not only
vis-à-vis the person experiencing the trauma as someone
who is suffering, but first and foremost as an "other"
in whose core experience there is something that goes
beyond the symbolic and political contours that purport
to represent him. And this turns him into a symbol
and manifestation of intense ethical commitment towards
radical otherness.

Bashir Bashir and Amos Goldberg, *The Holocaust and the Nakba: A New Grammar of Trauma and History*,
Columbia University Press, New York, 2018, p. 100–2.

public spheres — becomes the groundwork through which the relationship between German, Jewish and Arab histories can be approached in more complex and just ways retrospectively, now, and in the future. According to Rothberg, "[a]n ethics of multidirectional memory involves creating fidelity [...] with the multiple events and historical legacies that define any situation. A politics built on that ethical foundation will require a notion of transnational, comparative justice that can negotiate conflicting and sometimes mutually exclusive demands made on unstable and shifting terrain".[8]

Importantly, the resonances between different histories, the public traditions of memory that have developed around them and the disputes around calls for justice (what kind and for whom) bring us to what political philosopher Nancy Fraser calls "the politics of framing". Fraser argues that in a globalising world that has complicated the mandates of the Keynesian-Westphalian nation state, justice has three dimensions: economic redistribution, cultural recognition and political representation.[9] Though both economic and cultural dimensions are themselves political in that they are embedded in contested relations of power, Fraser defines the political as furnishing "the stage on which struggles over distribution and recognition are played out".[10] With the political as this site of articulation, Fraser emphasises the importance of the politics of framing: "Focused on the issues of who counts as the subject of justice, and what is the appropriate frame, the politics of framing comprises efforts to establish and consolidate, to contest and revise, the authoritative division of political space."[11] With Rothberg and Fraser there is a crucial paradigmatic shift in our collective conception of memory and justice, one that moves away from strictly national and *monologic* delineations to transnational, global and *dialogic* iterations.

The trilogy asks what it means to locate cinema at the intersection of these concerns and whether cinema has the potential of becoming an arena where the politics of framing might be articulated: What are the archival conditions for constructing the frame? Who are the subjects that can enter it and be recognised as historical actors? Which episodes from what contexts can be represented within it and by whom? Critically, might cinema be able to redistribute political space in such a way that it alters the foundations of the archive and the mechanisms of inclusions and exclusions that it sustains? Starting from the premise that cinema is a social

---

8    Rothberg, *Multidirectional Memory*, p. 22.
9    Nancy Fraser, "Reframing Justice in a Globalizing World", *New Left Review* 36, 2005, p. 70; Fraser explains that her use of the term "Keynesian-Westphalian" is meant to designate "the national-territorial underpinning of justice disputes" in the period from 1945 to the 1970s; while "Westphalian" refers to the main features of the international state system that emerged from the Treaty of Westphalia (1648), Fraser "invokes 'Westphalia' as a political imaginary that mapped the world as a system of mutually recognizing sovereign nation states" (footnote 2).
10   Fraser, "Reframing Justice in a Globalizing World", p. 79.
11   Fraser, p. 80.

apparatus that contributes to a constellation of biopolitical nervous systems, Gal addresses how its aesthetic and affective forms and force fields are active in operations of subjectivisation. The paradoxical challenge, then, is how to harness the field of visuality and its embodied archaeologies in order to create the foundations for multidirectional memory as a necessary corollary to constructing visions of justice. In other words, how might we disrupt those normative, dead-end visions offered by politicians and other actors who concretise and instrumentalise the past in monologic ways? Through a different form of visuality, shaped by a hallucinatory cinema, might we have dialogical visions of the future? For Gal, this entails complicating the demarcations between perpetrators and victims, engendering empathetic feelings for shared experiences of dispossession and violence, implicating the spectator as a constitutive participant in the making of meaning and considering how the relations between the seen and unseen have been produced by specific paradigms of knowledge. Critically, through a deliberate muddling of temporal, spatial and narrative structures that transform facticity and historicity into contradictory visual and phenomenological experiences, each film composes a singular material armature for a politics of framing.

## *WHITE CITY*:
## BECOMING A DIALOGIC PUBLIC OF MEMORY

Let's look at an example: *White City* opens with the successive presentation of two postcards, one depicting the Weißenhofsiedlung with a photomontage of Arab inhabitants produced by the Nazis circa 1934 that appeared in various German publications in the 1930s and 1940s with a caption reading "1940 Stuttgart. Weissenhofsiedlung, Araberdorf" (Arab village), and the other representing the brand-new modernist housing estate as it was originally exhibited in the summer of 1927.[12] These postcards function in multiple ways: First, as official press material and propaganda, they

12  The Weißenhofsiedlung near Stuttgart was sponsored by the Deutscher Werkbund and designed by Ludwig Mies van der Rohe in 1927. It included single-family apartments and housing designed by Le Corbusier, Peter Behrens, Bruno Taut, Walter Gropius, Hans Scharoun and other renowned architects, many of whom were proponents of the International Style. According to Thomas Elsaesser, the Weißenhofsiedlung's notoriety is linked to the anonymously produced photomontage that denounced modernism as an "Arab village", populated by camels, a lion and Bedouins. See Thomas Elsaesser, "The Architectural Postcard: Photography, Cinema, and Modernist Mass Media", *Grey Room* 70, 2018, p. 80–101. In endnote 2, p. 97, he writes: "The more common denunciation of the modern movement was to refer to its buildings as a 'Jerusalem suburb,' a phrase Paul Bonatz used when he attacked the Mies van der Rohe master plan for Weissenhof: 'In vielfältigen horizontalen Terrassierungen drängt sich in unwohnlicher Enge eine Häufung von flachen Kuben am Abhang hinauf, eher an eine Vorstadt Jerusalems erinnernd als an Wohnungen für Stuttgart' (A cluster of flat cubic volumes arranged in variegated terraces are packed in an uncomfortably narrow manner up against a hill, reminiscent more of a Jerusalem suburb than dwellings in Stuttgart). Paul Bonatz, "Noch einmal die Werkbundsiedlung", *Schwäbischer Merkur, Abendblatt*, 5 May 1926.

Dani Gal, *White City*, 2018, film still, camera: Itay Marom

Set photography, *White City*, 2018,
photo: Dani Gal

Dani Gal, *White City*, 2018, film still, camera: Itay Marom

affirm that the story we are about to witness exists simultaneously in the realms of fact and fiction. With this assertion, they also raise questions about the ways in which facticity is produced and critiqued through an authorial choice of visual angles, points of views and (avant-garde) strategies of photomontage. Second, they are the material arena for the performance of the pliability and mobility of time and space. Not only are they visual-textual missives sent to a contemporaneous addressee who lives at a spatial remove from the original locale and receives it as a reproduction, but they also exist as spaces of potentiality dispatched to anticipated readers and viewers in every possible future. In each case, the receiver of the postcard participates in generating the image's meaning in relation to a spectrum of visible and invisible frameworks. Third, the inextricability and mutual imbrication of whiteness — as a characteristic of modernist architecture — and degeneracy or "primitivism" — as fundamental tropes in the Nazi lexicon — emphasise the complexity of race as a biopolitical category linked to various ideologies, discourses and medias.[13] As a paradigmatic entry point to *White City*, these postcards thus function as archives that crystallise the constitution of multiple, nonsynchronous

13  The permutation of this binary logic between "whiteness" and "blackness" continues to organise hierarchies of power in the architectural construction of Tel Aviv in relation to Jaffa and the subsequent architectural narrative that organised the history of Israeli architecture. See Sharon Rotbard, *White City, Black City: Architecture and War in Tel Aviv and Jaffa* [2005], translated by Orit Gat, Pluto Press, London, 2015.

Dani Gal, *White City*, 2018, film still, camera: Itay Marom

*subjects who become publics* through the ongoing fabrication of multidirectional histories and memories.

In every scene, Gal punctures the monologic archive of the nation state by making visible the interlinked power relations embedded in modernist architecture and the discourses of race that emerged in the nineteenth and twentieth centuries. Turning over the official postcard of 1927, Arthur Ruppin writes to his wife, Hannah, about the modernist project in Stuttgart and its evocations of Richard Kauffmann's International Style in Palestine, thus connecting the aesthetics and ideologies of modernism in Europe and the Middle East. The film takes us through Ruppin's early support of "racial types", his practice of phrenology, and his exchange with Hans F. K. Günther about the "natural hierarchies" and eventual "refinement of races" (German Jewish as an apogee for Ruppin, and Nordic types for Günther).[14] While walking through the Weißenhofsiedlung, Ruppin notes, "Everything is foreign" (Alles ist Fremd), a remark repeated verbatim by one of his Jewish "scientific subjects" when he exhorts the man to fulfil his historical mission by moving from Europe to the Levant; eventually, this turn of phrase functions to link and delink Ruppin and Günther when the former characterises Hebrew as "very alien to the Aryan people" (Das Hebraisch ist Arysch sehr Fremd). In this merry-go-round of enunciation, we understand that the foreignness of the "other" is simultaneously

14  See Amos Morris-Reich, "Arthur Ruppin's Concept of Race", *Israel Studies* 11, no. 3, 2006, p. 1–30.

Dani Gal, *White City*, 2018, film stills, camera: Itay Marom

*dialogic*, i.e., related to and altered by previous texts and enunciations in a nonsynchronous way, and *contingent*, i.e., conditional on an embodied and situated point of view concomitant with particular regimes of knowledge. Moreover, as we follow the unfolding drama, we already know that the string of words, phrases and exchanges, which at times may seem innocuous, establishes the groundwork for an eventual violence or violence that has already been enacted. The film's last scene — observed from Ruppin's standpoint and accompanied by an electronic arabesque musical score — revisits the initial mise-en-scène of the Weißenhofsiedlung as visualised by those mid-century postcards but now with a truck transporting Arab inhabitants away. In this overlay of *dispositifs*, we are at once in Germany, Palestine and Israel negotiating the formation of modernism and otherness and its political instrumentalisation in the nervous system of interlaced transnational histories.

## *AS FROM AFAR*:
## BLUEPRINTS FOR MODELS,
## MEMORIES AND MEMORIALISATION

Another example: In *As from Afar*, the friendship between Simon Wiesenthal and Albert Speer explores different formulations, constructions and sensations of memory and the way they become condensed in images and material artifacts. Here, too, Gal uses a recurrent prop — i.e., the model — as a site through which to make visible the evidentiary conventions of memory production as it manifests in a simultaneous dynamic of verification, denial, repression and rewriting. In keeping with Gal's own dialogical strategies, allow me to narrate the first three minutes and ten seconds of the film in a sequence of short passages.

*One:*     In the establishing shot, which precedes the title of the film, the camera zooms closely onto the face of an elderly man — who we will soon learn is the model-maker Herr Kuck — while a male narrator, citing Ludwig Wittgenstein, asks us to consider the difference between "a memory image [...] that comes with an expectation" and "an image of a daydream". He continues, "You may be inclined to answer, 'There is an intrinsic difference between the images.' Did you notice that difference, or did you only say there was one because you thought there had to be one?"[15]

15   These musings are direct citations from Ludwig Wittgenstein's *Brown Book*, Section 25, first published in 1958 and based on notes that the philosopher had dictated to two of his students, Francis Skinner and Alice Ambrose, at Cambridge University during the academic year of 1934–35.

| | |
|---|---|
| *Two:* | Immediately after, we are virtually sutured to a sombre image of railway tracks wending their way between two towers while the accompanying soundtrack of wheels churning and creaking suggests a train in motion, and then, with gas hissing, arriving at a full stop. |
| *Three:* | Seen from above, we observe a workshop in which the model of the railway tracks and the wood scraps used to make it are amassed on a table while Wiesenthal, Speer and Herr Kuck stand around it in a triangular formation. The latter pulls the curtains open and turns off a spotlight in a performative gesture, as if to say, "The illusion is now revealed". Wiesenthal affirms: "The resemblance is striking", and, after a brief pause, starts narrating his memories of being a prisoner at Mauthausen. Another pause before he interjects: "But the railway track, there wasn't a railway track. I remember it exactly". He looks towards Speer and then asks, "There wasn't a track, was there?" To which Herr Kuck responds, "I built it for a big film production. Americans. They want railway tracks. They say otherwise it won't look like a concentration camp." Speer then inquires, "Where did you get the blueprints for the camp?" and Herr Kuck responds, "Blueprints? I didn't have any. I built it from memory". |

In this short sequence accompanied by Wittgenstein's preamble, Gal brings to the fore different *blueprints of memory* — philosophical, literary, cinematic, musical, architectural and personal — and asks us to consider their possible confluence and distribution in different cognitive ecologies. As the three men assemble in the workshop, they each have a singular relation to the memory and memorialisation of Mauthausen. If Herr Kuck built the model from personal memory, then Wiesenthal's own flood of memories are triggered by examining it, in spite of its flaws. Wanting to transmit these memories — both individual and collective — to future generations in a public forum, Wiesenthal incorporates the façade of Mauthausen in a proposal for a Holocaust memorial in Jerusalem. Meanwhile, we realise that memories and their afterlives are simultaneously manufactured by a film industry that has consolidated certain referents as signifying the Holocaust, like the mandatory railway tracks, regardless of historical veracity.[16] In contrast, we know from historical

---

16 Griselda Pollock and Max Silverman note that the capitalised term Holocaust "became a widely used name for the attempted destruction of European Jewry between 1941 and 1945 only after the mid-1950s. [It] was effectively consolidated in Euro-American popular cultural memory by its use as the title of an American TV series about the destruction of Jewish Germans, *Holocaust*, created by Gerald Green in 1978, and watched by millions of people in the United States and across Europe". See *Concentrationary Cinema: Aesthetics as Political Resistance in Alain Resnais's* Night and Fog, Berghahn, Oxford, 2012, p. 3.

Dani Gal, *As from Afar*, 2013, film still, camera: Emre Erkmen

Simon Wiesenthal, architectural sketch, circa 1948

Drawing of the entrance gate to Mauthausen concentration camp as it is depicted in the draft of the mausoleum proposed by Wiesenthal for a Holocaust memorial. Wiesenthal hoped the memorial would be built in Jerusalem, but the plans were never actualised.

Set photography, *As from Afar*, 2013, photo: Emre Erkmen

Dani Gal, *As from Afar*, 2013, film stills, camera: Emre Erkmen

sources that Speer's visit to Mauthausen in spring 1943 and his demand that the labour of all prisoners be mobilised towards arms production, often in underground tunnel systems, effectively intensified the death rate at the complex and its subcamps.[17] Later on in Gal's film, however, when asked by Wiesenthal if he had ever been to Mauthausen, Speer responds that he had been there once, "if he remembers correctly", a statement put into question by a newspaper clipping with the headline "Mauthausen war Idee von Speer" (Mauthausen was Speer's idea) that Wiesenthal carries in his pocket but does not show Speer.

With these performative assertions, conjectures and repudiations — some spoken and others remaining silent — we understand that the blueprint for personal and collective memory depends on who has built it, in which context and for what purpose. At the same time, we observe how all of the actors on this historical stage are somehow *possessed* by memory as a subjective and social practice that can neither be mastered nor owned by any one of them. The awareness that we are all still living in a haunted house that keeps dialogically reproducing its legacies of trauma, Gal suggests, serves as the constitutive groundwork for continuing to work through shared histories.

## *NIGHT AND FOG*:
## MEMORY AS LIVING TESTIMONY

Unlike the other two films in the trilogy, *Night and Fog* is narrated entirely from the perspective of the main protagonist, Michael Goldman-Gilad. Basing the re-enactment of the secret mission to scatter Eichmann's ashes beyond the territorial limits of the State of Israel on an almost verbatim interview with Goldman-Gilad, Gal emphasises the convergences between historical testimony, memory and storytelling.[18] The drama begins visually with a nod to the tropes of film noir — stark lighting and deep shadows, extreme high-angle shots and taught dialogue — as Goldman-Gilad recounts how he came to take part in the unfolding events. His narrative is framed by the broader context of the Eichmann trial, which we learn "gave many survivors a unique opportunity to talk about what they had gone through. They were able to share stories that they had kept to themselves for nearly two decades". Citing both the Nacht und Nebel directive issued by Hitler on 4 December 1941 by which any opponent

---

17 "Forced Labour in the Arms Industry" and "Relocating arms production underground" (undated articles), webpages retrieved from https://www.mauthausen-memorial.org/.

18 Interview with Michael Goldman-Gilad in Israel, February 2010, personal research archive of Dani Gal; see also Michael Goldman-Gilad's interview conducted by Limor Bar-Ilan and Yael Novogrodsky for Yad Vashem – The World Holocaust Remembrance Center in Jerusalem, https://www.yadvashem.org/articles/interviews/goldman-gilad.html.

of the National Socialist regime could be clandestinely disappeared, and Alain Resnais's film *Nuit et brouillard*, the seminal documentary about the Holocaust that alternates between past and present, Gal's film enacts the liminal space of memory that hovers between silence and speech. Storytelling — or telling your story publicly as a historical imperative — is performed as a process of fractured yet tangled temporalities that stand in contrast with cinematographic realism. Bracketed within the single night of Eichmann's cremation yet speaking from the perspective of the present, Goldman-Gilad chronicles his involvement in the case as an adult and his survival of the Holocaust as an adolescent. With three different timelines continually at play, there is an uneasy traffic between the storyteller's memories and the conventions of realistic representations that pushes the narrative-image overlay out of sync.

Case in point: the first scene unfolds during the night of 1 June 1962 as a gurney is wheeled away and a furnace guarded by policemen still smoulders. Goldman-Gilad takes us back to Eichmann's capture in Argentina in 1960, and then two years prior, to 1958, when he had left his job as police investigator. Looping back, he narrates his return to the force in 1960 when Eichmann was brought to Israel and his request to be assigned to Bureau 06 in order to gather evidence for the trial that would take place a year later, between 11 April and 15 December 1961. With the image of the furnace still dominating the screen and Goldman-Gilad's memories meandering, we hear of his first encounter with Eichmann: "He looked miserable to me, he wasn't wearing a belt and his shoelaces and his false teeth had been removed. But when he opened his mouth, I felt as if I were standing at the open gates to the crematorium."

The juxtaposition of the Holocaust survivor's memories of Auschwitz-Birkenau with an image depicting the cremation of the Nazi perpetrator is jarring. It becomes all the more powerful when we realise that Goldman-Gilad's violent flashback occurs as he faces his former persecutor during the investigation with the power dynamics between them reversed. More so, it is seeing Eichmann's mouth that provokes his hallucination: speaking is a matter of life and death for both survivor and perpetrator. The survivor is a living witness, speaking in the name of justice for those who were murdered, while the perpetrator is speaking in order to remain alive and evade justice. The dialogical relationship between these two figures is triangulated by the implicit presence of the film's spectator, who is interpellated as a contributor to the politics of framing. Imagined as a possible member of a political community who brings a specific archive of knowledge to bear, the spectator may be stimulated to reflect on how their own situated viewpoint impacts their understanding of the still dominant national model that has established the German-Jewish dyad as unique and somehow unrelated to other struggles.

The Eichmann trial in Jerusalem gave many survivors a unique opportunity to talk about what they had gone through. They were able to share stories that they had kept to themselves for nearly two decades. Only in the presence of a judge, people began to listen: on one occasion, the court projected documentary films of the concentration camps and replaced the film soundtracks with the live commentary of the witnesses. This strangely took the courtroom back to the silent film era.

Dani Gal, *Night and Fog*, opening slide, 2011

Screening of *Nazi Concentration Camp* during the trial of Adolf Eichmann, Beit Ha'am, Jerusalem, 1961

Dani Gal, *Night and Fog*, 2011, film still, camera: Itay Marom

Set photography, *Night and Fog*, 2011,
photo: Michal Baror

If we extend this consideration beyond the immediate frame of *Night and Fog*, we might ask more pointedly: How has the State of Israel, which was largely formed as a response to the Holocaust, become a perpetrator through its occupation of the Palestinian people and their lands? And what happens to our understanding of the Holocaust if it is comparatively connected to other twentieth-century genocides, such as the mass killings of Armenians carried out in Turkey and adjoining regions, the massacre of Bosniaks in Srebrenica or the slaughter of Tutsis in Rwanda? With lives shaped by national identifications, supranational institutions and sociopolitical, financial and technological processes that extend beyond territorial borders, what is the grammar for our contemporary notion of justice and human rights, our criteria of social belonging or the parameters for the entitlement to recognition within the category of humanity?

## CONCLUSION: HALLUCINATORY CINEMA

The archive of modernity, Gal suggests, is full of quotidian moments, speech acts and images in which we are at once inside and outside the frame, looking at the past with a sense of belonging or unbelonging, identification or disidentification. As spectators of a hallucinatory cinema, we are urged to ask: Are we the claimants of this past? Is it part of our commons? And, crucially, how do we unlearn the monologic paradigms of knowledge that this modern archive has established? Each of Gal's films brings into visibility seminal events that have not yet entered a collective dialogical archive of multidirectional memory. This is not necessarily because they were not known, as Ruppin and Günther's exchanges, Wiesenthal and Speer's friendship and Goldman-Gilad's testimony are all well-established. Rather, for many years, it remained difficult — because of a dominant organisation of knowledge — to connect between German and Jewish histories in empathetic ways or to interrogate the ways in which the Zionist project, as linked to the establishment of the State of Israel, has violently affected both Palestinian and Jewish populations by creating the conditions in which they have respectively been constituted as victims and perpetrators by a military logic.[19] Indeed, despite the transnational pulses of globalisation that have reshaped some aspects of the Keynesian-Westphalian nation state, the power of this modern political structure and its archives remains in place. It has even intensified in recent years, continually reproduced in the biopolitical nervous system of

---

19  See Ariella Azoulay, "Potential History: Thinking through Violence", *Critical Inquiry* 39, no. 3, 2013, p. 548–74.

its subjects. It is extremely difficult to step out of the seemingly fixed roles and positions ascribed to us as subjects of history and memory within the parameters of nation states and imagine other options. Yet we also know that during these recalcitrant times of renewed racism, anti-Semitism and xenophobia, it is all the more pressing to bring to the fore those dialogical dimensions of history that have been buried or overlooked, as well as a politics of framing that is linked to multidimensional memory. Hallucinatory cinema, emerging from the mimetic order that has long organised the facticity and historicity of the real, makes images and bodies vibrate from within and causes nervous systems to tremble.

But we can also read the address of the voice here, not as the story of the individual in relation to the events of his own past, but as the story of the way in which one's own trauma is tied up with the trauma of another, the way in which trauma may lead, therefore, to the encounter with another, through the very possibility of surprise of listening to another's wound.

Cathy Caruth, *Unclaimed Experience: Trauma, Narrative, and History*, Johns Hopkins University Press, Baltimore, 1996, p. 8.

The category of multidirectional memory allows us to begin to approach the simultaneously political and psychic nature of the excess in such discourses because it insists that we take seriously the crosscutting nature of public memories. While memory wars such as those that continue to roil the Middle East can provoke despair at the reduction of politics to crude stereotypes and name calling, the uncomfortable proximity of memories is also the cauldron out of which new visions of solidarity and justice must emerge. [...] I draw two corollaries from the kinds of memory conflicts emblematized by the Israeli/Palestinian dispute. First, we cannot stem the structural multidirectionality of memory. Even if it were desirable — as it sometimes seems to be — to maintain a wall, or *cordon sanitaire*, between different histories, it is not possible to do so. Memories are mobile; histories are implicated in each other. Thus, finally, understanding political conflict entails understanding the interlacing of memories in the force field of public space. The only way forward is through their entanglement.

Michael Rothberg, *Multidirectional Memory: Remembering the Holocaust in the Age of Decolonization*, Stanford University Press, Stanford, 2009, p. 313.

# IN CONVERSATION
## Sabeth Buchmann with Dani Gal

SABETH BUCHMANN    To get straight into the complex subjects of your films, I was asking myself how to grasp their really extreme perspectives. Your trilogy deals with very different episodes of Jewish history and the diaspora and the Shoah respectively. Their programmatic common denominator lies in the concept of "multidirectional memory" — a crucial reference here is Michael Rothberg's 2009 book — a research direction that is more present than ever due to the current debates about the reframing of anti-Semitism and the Shoah. At a time when "decolonisation" is becoming a central component of historical and cultural research, as well as anthropology and ethnology, can it be said that your artistic interest is situated through an active participation in corresponding historiographical and epistemological shifts, which has helped determine their respective forms? For example: What could be the reason for the aerial perspective at the beginning of *Night and Fog* that is slightly *schreck* (frightening) or displaced, which gives the whole scene a literally meta-reflexive atmosphere?

DANI GAL                *Night and Fog* opens with a long shot from the perspective of the prison guard, from the point of view of the perpetrator. Based on cinematic conventions, I wanted to establish a type of cinematic Shoah imagery right from the start. I wanted the viewer to experience immediate recognition but realise after a few seconds that it is actually not the Shoah because the uniforms do not match. These are Israeli police

Dani Gal, *Night and Fog*, 2011, film still, camera: Itay Marom

officers guarding the furnace burning Eichmann's body in a prison yard in Israel. The viewer watches one reality while associating it with another.

SB    In order to prepare for our discussions, I went back to *Bilder trotz allem* (*Images in Spite of All*) by Georges Didi-Huberman. It is very interesting how he elaborates upon the conflict with his critics and with Claude Lanzmann. The question of whether it is possible to understand those images of concentration camps as "aesthetic gestures" or "Bildakte" (image acts), as images that are able to actually represent an action, is not resolved. While reading *Bilder trotz allem* and another text on the reception of the book, I came across a statement by Jean-Luc Godard where he says "there is a missing link in the representation"; this then made a click in my head, and I thought that it could be the question of perspective. What Didi-Huberman explains is the point of view of the Sonderkommandos (special commandos), the Jewish prisoners who were involved in the murderous machinery in the concentration camps, through a camera that was smuggled in and out of Auschwitz-Birkenau.

DG    It reminds me of the French documentary *Sous le Manteau* (*Clandestinely*) from 1948 that contains footage shot by French prisoners of war in a camp in Austria during the Second World War. The prisoners installed a camera inside a Larousse dictionary and used film that was smuggled in with the food supply.

SB    Didi-Huberman speculates about two images taken from a camera hidden at the bottom of a bucket. He speaks of the "terrible paradoxe de cette *chambre noire* [dark chamber]".[1] I paraphrase: In order to use the camera, the photographer, a Greek-Jewish man named Alex, had to hide in the gas chamber — i.e., he had to hide in the dark, in obscurity, between these recordings. The art historian states that the photos document the daily work of the Sonderkommandos and the SS. He can only speculate how many other recordings were made with the camera. Alex did take more photographs: In front of the birch forest, where a group of undressed women are on their way to the gas chamber, he encounters some SS officers. Since the photos are shaky and out of position, Didi-Huberman speculates that Alex took them without looking, maybe even without stopping. But that is how he captures the perpetrators' perspective. It seems clear that the camera was returned to another member of the Sonderkommonado, David Szmulewski, who was observing the SS men from a roof. According to Didi-Huberman, the whole action lasted fifteen to twenty minutes. Szmulewski again hid the camera in the bucket and handed it over to Helena Datón, an employee of the SS canteen, who transported the film strip in a toothpaste tube out of Auschwitz-Birkenau, where it came into the hands of the Polish resistance in Kraków. One of the central theses is that the normality of everyday camp life reflects the perspective of the perpetrators, whose job was to dematerialise the bodies of their victims.

DG    Lanzmann took an extreme position against evidence from the camps when he said, "If I had discovered a hypothetical silent film shot by an SS officer showing the deaths of 3,000 people in a gas chamber, not only would I not have included it in my film, I would have destroyed it".[2]

SB    Yes, exactly, for him the photos evidently have no legitimate existence.

DG    For Godard, it is the missing image that he is looking for as a film maker; for Lanzmann, it is an image that can only exist in the head of the listener of the testimony, which is both the filmmaker and the viewer. The history of cinema is full of failed attempts at representing historical events.

SB    Godard also addresses it as a fantasy. The perpetrators' perspective on their daily routine of eliminating the battered bodies should not exist;

1    George Didi-Huberman, *Images malgré tout*, Édition de Minuit, Paris, p. 22.
2    Claude Lanzmann, *The Patagonian Hare: A Memoir* [2009], trans. Frank Wynne, Atlantic Books, London, 2012, p. 898.

thus it positions the image beyond valid representation. The (re-)production and (re-)presentation of structurally impossible images by and of the victims is made impossible a second time.

DG    This brings to mind Dori Laub's claim that the Shoah was an event without a witness because of the efforts to destroy the possibility of witnessing it from within or from without. When I interviewed Michael Goldman-Gilad during my research for *Night and Fog*, he told me that as a very young man, his job at Auschwitz was to scatter human ashes over the walking paths to prevent people from slipping on the ice during the winter. He said that when he looked at the mountain of ashes, he tried to understand how many people it summed up to. Later, he said the milk jug that contained Eichmann's ashes was less than half full. A human body is about four hundred grams of ashes. It is not much. It was Goldman-Gilad himself who scattered Eichmann's ashes into the Mediterranean Sea to eliminate any evidence of the body. That night can be seen as a symbolic act of Shoah enacted on one person in terms of the technical procedure. First of all, the state changed the law to introduce capital punishment, and following the trial, they acquired the technology of body burning. The burning of the body is forbidden in Judaism. Lastly, they eliminated the remnants of the body.

    The origin story of the furnace that was used to burn Eichmann's body has a few different versions. One version claims that the furnace came from the Israeli cement factory Nesher, which means eagle, or *Adler* in German. Another went so far as to claim that the furnace came from Germany. For the film, I chose the version about a thirteen-year-old kid who worked at an oven factory in Israel. He was instructed to build the furnace and was told that it was for burning fish bones. This factory was owned by Amichai Paglin, a former member of the Irgun, who was known for his involvement in numerous terror attacks against the British Mandate. In 1972, Paglin was also involved in illegal weapon smuggling together with a far-right Jewish organisation in an attempt to commit a terror attack in Libya as revenge for the massacre during the Summer Olympics in Munich. There is a small museum for the Irgun, the Zionist paramilitary organisation named after Paglin. The museum is built on top of the destruction of Menashiya, which was a Palestinian neighbourhood in Jaffa before 1948.

SB    Your remarks already reveal the core of your project and of your working method: A combination of different perspectives, which, among other things, consists of a reversal of the perpetrator-victim relationship. Following Michael Rothberg, multidirectional memory challenges the competition that can exist between memories in regards to which ones are chronicled for the foundational constitution of a national identity or of a social group. This brings up certain questions: How can we integrate the perspectives of the others into our own perception and awareness? How can we relate to the memories of the others? And how far can we also reconsider the Shoah into the history of colonisation? I would argue that to say there is a legacy of oppression going further back in history is never meant to relativise the specificity of the Shoah, but instead, a decolonial reading can help to contextualise it.

DG   The argument against relativising the Shoah has that competitive element. In essence, it is a claim for the worst and greatest catastrophe and as a result suggests that all other state violence is tolerable. This status has given the State of Israel justification for the ongoing violence and dispossession of Palestinians. There is a brutal and cynical instrumentalisation of the Shoah and its memory. Heterogeneity always existed among people, but when the nation state imposes a homogenous identity, some narratives are suppressed in favour of others. This is why multidirectional memory is very important as a political idea. It proposes taking the historical narrative away from power, from the nation state and from representation that serves a national agenda.

SB   From a left-wing German perspective, it is difficult for me to relativise the Shoah. Although I wouldn't want to grant the Germans the privilege of being unique in their acts of genocide, the acknowledgement of state-organised industrial murder does play an important role in how I think about Germany's historical commitment to the victims of Nazi terror.

DG   Each historical trauma is unique and needs to be acknowledged as specific to the people who suffered or are suffering from it. It is not about comparison; it is about acceptance. The perpetrators are not free from trauma either and I believe that this needs to be acknowledged too. There is no moral dimension to trauma. If German soldiers suffered from trauma as a result of the Second World War, it is a real trauma, it is a trauma that exists in the German society, which is different from the trauma that exists in the Israeli society, and different from the trauma that exist in the Palestinian society. And Palestinians still suffer from ongoing state violence and dispossession as we speak.

SB   I understand your plea for a multi-perspective approach in view of recent historical research and the reflection on nationalist instrumentalisation of the Shoah for nationalist purposes. Referring to what we said before about Godard's fantasy: Do your cinematic means meet this approach in allowing us, the viewers, to inhabit previously unperceived perspectives?

DG    I try to destabilise the binarism between victims and perpetrators to allow a discussion about previously unperceived perspectives. For example, the real prison where Eichmann was held and executed and the film location used for the prison scenes in *Night and Fog* are both Tegart forts. These compounds are named after Charles Tegart, who was a British colonial police officer in India who specialised in counterinsurgency against indigenous people. Following the 1936 Arab Revolt against British colonial rule in Palestine following the establishment of an open immigration policy for Jewish people, Tegart was sent to Palestine to contain the uprising. He recommended building these militarised police forts to protect the counterinsurgents. After 1948, with the establishment of the State of Israel, these forts became police stations and prisons, some of which are operational to this day.

SB    In other words, you relate the location of your case study — the traceless removal of Eichmann's ashes — to the historical context of colonialism and its consequences for the Palestinians. Does this also imply a re-historicisation of Shoah memory?

DG    By pointing at the architectural locations of the original prison and the film location of it, I contextualise the Eichmann affair within the context of colonialism to show that the two histories, the aftermath of the Shoah and its consequences for the Palestinians, are interwoven in a way that cannot be undone. This point also comes forward at the end of *Night and Fog* when the police boat — on its way back from scattering Eichmann's ashes — crosses two Palestinian fishermen from Jaffa who are going out to sea. The fishermen look at them, questioning suspiciously their activities at sea. At this moment, the two histories look each other straight in the eyes, as the Israeli poet Avot Yeshurun eloquently put it.

SB    The architecture is of significant importance also for the Eichmann trial, which is mentioned in the opening slide of your film. In her book, *Eichmann in Jerusalem: A Report on the Banality of Evil*, Hannah Arendt describes the courtroom as a theatre, which resonates in the set design of *Night and Fog*. Here, it creates an alienation effect reminiscent of Bertolt Brecht, who reminds us that representation always implies fiction. Following Arendt, the historical witnesses, who were also the victims testifying in court, also represented the audience in a trial that David Ben-Gurion, the Israeli prime minister at the time, wished to work like a spectacle. Since your concept opts for multidirectional memory and

Tegart fort in Abu Ghosh, Israel, film location of *Night and Fog*, 2011, photo: Michal Baror

Police Tegart fort in Iraq Suwaydan, Mandatory Palestine, circa 1948

Dani Gal, *Night and Fog*, 2011, film still, camera: Itay Marom

Reconstruction of a colonial British police interrogation room in a Tegart fort
in Mandatory Palestine, Ma'alot-Tarshiha Police Station Museum, Israel,
photo: Yaron Kaminsky

empathy on the part of the audience, does it have the potential to cause more distance from the historical processing of the Nazi crimes?

DG  The courtroom that was used for the Eichmann trial was in fact a theatre and still functions as one; the theatricality was there from the start. This brings to mind Arendt's concept of the actor/spectator: the clash between the reflective judgment of the actor and the philosophical judgment of the spectator. In the trilogy, I constantly move between immersive cinematic techniques to a more theatrical setting, and even documentary techniques at times, so that the viewer shifts from being pulled into the film to being pushed out to a critical position, thus moving between being an actor and a spectator. When you say that my methodology could cause more distance from the historical processing of Nazi crimes, do you mean the possibility for redemption?

SB  No, I don't want to speak of redemption. But what does it mean to enter, as a consequence, into a relationship of empathy with the perpetrator?

DG  The game of changing perspectives is about the attempt to liberate the viewer from dichotomies and look at the behaviour of humans under extreme conditions, or at least to suggest such extreme perspectives. I think forgiveness is another very important perspective.

SB  That's the radical key point in your work, also in your second film, *As from Afar*, in which you construct an encounter between Albert Speer and Simon Wiesenthal: A dialogue between perpetrator and victim, or between several respective groups of victims. It is a form of bringing each specific memory into interrelated interaction.

DG  The case of Wiesenthal is interesting in the context of addressing the possibility of forgiveness. By dedicating his life to bringing Nazi criminals to justice, he got very close to them until he crossed the assumed ethical boundary between victims and perpetrators by having a close relationship with Speer.

SB  Is your staging of their encounter once again an interpretation in the spirit of Rothberg?

DG  I read Rothberg's *Multidirectional Memory* after I made the films, but it is indeed a very useful concept with which to address their relationship, as I mentioned earlier. At the time of making *As from Afar* and *Night and Fog*, my motivation was rooted in an attempt to represent the aftermath of the Shoah and its memory in a more complex way than the cinematic representation I was exposed to. One of the concepts that I had at the back of my mind was Primo Levi's "gray zone", where he describes the collapse of a clear dichotomy between good and evil in the reality of the concentration camps. Especially in *As from Afar*, I try to question the nature of such representations and the forces behind them, national or economic.

SB    And is this also the reason why you choose Ludwig Wittgenstein from *The Brown Book* that features in *As from Afar*? I ask because the text seems to be the key to the process as well as to the content of the film, which complicates, of course, memory as a site of certainty.

DG    I used parts of his text as a voice-over, which functions as the narrator for the film. The voice also gives the text a philosophical meta-layer. The questions proposed by Wittgenstein articulate the essence of the trilogy. It asks how one can represent the past and how this representation is perceived by others. Are these images of a memory or of a dream? This is a question that is closely related to the essay by Noit Banai about hallucinatory cinema and the kind of images received by viewers in relation to their expectations while watching the films. Wittgenstein proposes the following exercise:

> Consider this example: What is the difference between a memory image, an image that comes with expectation, and say, an image of a daydream. You may be inclined to answer, "There is an intrinsic difference between the images". — Did you notice that difference, or did only you say there was one because you thought there must be one? [...] I will examine one particular case, that of a feeling which I shall roughly describe by saying it is the feeling of 'long, long ago'. These words and the tone in which they are said are a gesture of pastness. But I will specify the experience which I mean still further by saying that it is corresponding to a certain tune (Davids Bündler Tänze — "Wie aus weiter Ferne"). I'm imagining this tune played with the right expression and thus recorded, say, for a gramophone. Then this is the most elaborate and exact expression of a feeling of pastness which I can imagine.[3]

The gesture of pastness is not only the words chosen but also the way they are said, or in the case of a film, the manner in which the subject matter is depicted, including all of the formal decisions I made as a director.

3    Ludwig Wittgenstein, *The Blue and Brown Books: Preliminary Studies for the "Philosophical Investigations"*, Harper Perennial, New York, 1965, p. 182–84.

Dani Gal, *As from Afar*, 2013, film still, camera: Emre Erkmen

When recording the soundtrack for the film, I asked the pianist to play the piece by Robert Schumann four times, to play it differently each time. And each time, to try and transfer this feeling of pastness.

SB   Wittgenstein's concept of repetition implies the idea of working through the pastness; as such, it reminds us of a psychoanalytical topic, but Wittgenstein differentiates between the feeling of pastness and the expression of the feeling of pastness. What exactly does this difference mean for you?

DG   For me, in the context of the film this part of Wittgenstein's text relates to working with actors. Actors move between the feeling and the expression of the feeling. There are different techniques of acting. Some actors really try to feel as if the situation is real in order to express, and others express through a rational analysis of the situation of the character in a scene.

SB   It occurred to me that there is a conceptual gap between the way they act and what they say — a gap that never closes. Seeing the film through Wittgenstein's differentiation between the feeling of pastness and the expression of the feeling of pastness, the question arises whether this gap also applies to the perception of the individual figures as both concrete actors and allegorical representations of historical contexts.

The ascent of the privileged, not only in the Lager but in all human coexistence, is an anguishing but unfailing phenomenon: only in utopias it is absent. […] Where power is exercised by few or only one against the many, privilege is born and proliferates, even against the will of the power itself. On the other hand, it is normal for power to tolerate and encourage privilege. Let us confine ourselves to the Lager, which (even in its Soviet version) can be considered an excellent "laboratory": the hybrid class of the prisoner-functionary constitutes its armature and at the same time its most disquieting feature. It is a gray zone, poorly defined, where the two camps of masters and servants both diverge and converge. This gray zone possesses an incredibly complicated internal structure and contains within itself enough to confuse our need to judge.

Primo Levi, *The Drowned and the Saved* [1986], trans. Raymond Rosenthal, Simon & Schuster, New York, 2017, p. 31.

How does this relate, for example, to the stage designer Herr Kuck, who interacts with Wiesenthal and Speer at the beginning of *As from Afar*?

DG    Herr Kuck can see the entire event from above. He is the narrator. This is related to the idea of alternating between being inside a model and looking at a model from above, or from afar. The film ends when he is putting the final touches on a model of Haus Wittgenstein, right after Speer and Wiesenthal have been walking around, lost inside the real house in Vienna. Earlier in the film, we also see the two protagonists from inside of Herr Kuck's CCTV monitor. He has an ominous presence.

SB    Is the storyteller the one who imagines the story that is being told? In other words, is he the immanent narrator who transforms history or the representation of history into a more or less subjective narration?

DG    Maybe the answer for this unfolds in the first scene when Herr Kuck tells Speer that he did not build the model of the Mauthausen concentration camp from blueprints but based on his own memory. But we are never told when and in what capacity he was there, possibly as a prisoner.

SB    Later on, Wiesenthal and Speer are walking around on an outdoor film studio sound stage, so a conceivable reading is that the film is experienced through Herr Kuck's perspective.

DG    The establishing shot of *As from Afar* adopts the point of view of a train that is entering a concentration camp on a winter night. I based it on the iconic shot from Lanzmann's film *Shoah*, the point of view of a train entering Auschwitz-Birkenau. I realised that it has become an image that falsely represents the victim's point of view, although none of the victims could have had this point of view because they were in cattle cars with little or no view.

SB    Isn't it the point of view of the perpetrators? You visually quote this so-called icon of horror that is already inscribed into the collective memory.

DG    It could be the point of view of the perpetrators but this is challenged in *Shoah* when Lanzmann interviews the driver of the train line to Treblinka, who says that he didn't pull the wagons — he pushed them from the rear, so this point of view is probably not even of the driver. It is a fabrication that has become iconic in its representation of entering the horror. You can find many similar images on the internet in relation to concentration camp history. And it is this cinematic construction of re-

Dani Gal, *Model for a film set of the Mauthausen concentration camp drawn from the memory of Mr. Kuck*, 2013, detail, mixed media, 180 × 500 × 145 cm, installation view: Kunst Halle Sankt Gallen, 2013

Dani Gal, *Model for a film set of the Mauthausen concentration camp drawn from the memory of Mr. Kuck*, 2013, detail, mixed media, 180 × 500 × 145 cm, installation view: Jewish Museum, New York, 2013

Film crew during the shooting of Alain Resnais's *Nuit et brouillard* near Auschwitz-Birkenau, 1955

membrance that gave me the idea of using the Mauthausen model to serve as a prop in my film. The sculpture resembles a miniature model of the gates to Mauthausen, but when you look closer you can see that it is only a miniature film set for a night scene. There is a miniature camera on the train tracks like in the production shot of Alain Resnais's *Nuit et brouillard* (*Night and Fog*). Again, I ask the viewers to move between being above and being inside. When I installed the film with the sculpture, I always made sure that the visitors would see the model immediately after they came out of the screening room. This way they find themselves moving from the position of looking over the protagonists who are looking over the model from afar, to inhabiting the point of view of the protagonists in my film.

SB    That is a very interesting point. The trilogy is grounded within the procedures and mechanisms of cinematic memory that frame historical narration as something you cannot decouple from imagination and projection, working at the same time as objective frames.

DG    I am interested in how cinema is shaping our memories of historical events, events that we mainly remember through a cinematic construction. Most people who would watch a film that depicts a historical event never lived the event, but even those who did may have not experienced it this way. It is again the movement between above and within. When thinking critically about a film that depicts a historical event, like the Shoah, the authenticity question often comes up: How true is the film to the historical reality? I would like to ask the opposite: How true is the event to us? Because I only experienced it through representations, and representations are always subjective and therefore false. The process of making a film based on historical events is, in and of itself, a process of distortion.

SB    Does this resonate in the dialectic between the inside and outside view that your film performs by letting us watch the scene from above, from outside, from inside? Perception simultaneously becomes subject to a labyrinthine dissociation, which begins the moment the two men enter Haus Wittgenstein. Their movements struck me as allegorical of a disorientation of time and space.

DG    They are trapped, and they don't know how to get out.

SB    I found that the way the windows are filmed is spooky. They increase the feeling of disorientation and evoke the impression of being locked up, as if the outside were a phantasm and the two protagonists were imprisoned.

Dani Gal, *As from Afar*, 2013, film still, camera: Emre Erkmen

DG   I placed them in the house and filmed them as they get lost in it as if they are trapped in the labyrinth of language, which reflects directly back to the complexities of their dialogue. It is also a continued play with Wittgenstein's architectural metaphors of language. But Wittgenstein can also be very hermetic and sometimes not understandable at all.

SB   It is interesting that you say that. Wittgenstein is considered one of the protagonists of logical positivism, whose analytical philosophy of language was essential for the attempt of early linguistic conceptual art to establish a new, transparent ontology of art beyond the formalistic concepts of painting and sculpture.

DG   The last part of the voice-over is also from Wittgenstein's text: "I am inclined to suggest to you to put the expression of our experience in place of the experience."[4] It functions as a comment about the acting since actors do not possess the experience, although they can express it.

SB   The performance itself transforms the way memory is experienced…

4   Wittgenstein, *The Blue and Brown Books,* p. 184.

Dani Gal, *As from Afar*, 2013, film still, camera: Emre Erkmen

DG    Wittgenstein continues: "'But these two aren't the same'. This is certainly true, at least in the sense in which it is true to say that a railway and a railway accident aren't the same thing."[5] Of course, they are not the same, so why does he ask this question? In the context of the film, it throws the viewer back to the beginning, to the point of view from the train and the discussion from the first scene about the railway tracks that were added because the model is a commission for a Hollywood film and therefore needs railway tracks in order to become a credible representation of a concentration camp. Mauthausen did not have a railway.

SB    That is an interesting point. I see a strange analogy between the railway tracks and the window designs of Haus Wittgenstein that connects the fictional visit of Speer und Wiesenthal with their walk along the rails.

DG    The walks in the streets were filmed on the soundstage of the Bavaria film studios. It is a fake German city made only of façades. I wanted to show that it is a fake city. It is almost as if they are walking through a dead European city, to give the feeling of emptied houses — the void after a genocide. And of course, I also wanted to have them walk inside of a model. During the first scene at the model builder's atelier, Speer

5    Wittgenstein, p. 184.

tells an anecdote, which is historically true, that he once built a 1:1 façade for Hermann Wilhelm Göring's future palace, a building in Berlin that was never built. While he tells the story, the viewer can see him through the back side of the Mauthausen model, which reveals itself to be only a façade.

SB    There is also the visual quotation of *The Night Porter* by Liliana Cavani, a film depicting the sadomasochistic relationship between a former concentration camp victim and a former Nazi perpetrator. Is this reference a commentary on the nature of the relationship or interactions between Wiesenthal and Speer?

DG    I was thinking of *The Night Porter* for several reasons. The sadomasochistic love affair between the SS officer and the Jewish female prisoner started in Mauthausen; the two characters meet years later in Vienna. Wiesenthal was a prisoner in Mauthausen and Speer allegedly initiated the construction of the camp; Wiesenthal also meets Speer in Vienna. The dynamic between my protagonists has a psychological dimension with certain sadomasochistic aspects. The victim and the perpetrator are both attracted to each other in order to redeem themselves, but at the same time, they take advantage of each other for their own interests and suspect one another. While reading the letters exchanged between Wiesenthal and Speer, I understood that there are multiple reasons why the two became close friends, but it is not clear to me how genuine this friendship was.

SB    The two men even speak about Hitler's infernal hatred towards Jewish people and link it to an encounter with a Jewish sex worker from whom he got syphilis.

DG    It is one of the questions that Wiesenthal asks Speer in the first letter. It is really bizarre but also typical of an eccentric, rough and very direct character like Wiesenthal. It is a strange question because it sounds as if he diminishes the magnitude of the crime of the Shoah and society's acceptance of the genocide, as if Hitler hated Jewish people for such a personal, immature reason.

SB    Your decision to locate the encounter in Vienna seems also crucial. After the war, Wiesenthal was not a well-respected person in Austria, a country that denied responsibility for its involvement in Nazi crimes. This becomes thematised in your film when we read from the newspaper clipping in the hands of the Wiesenthal character that Mauthausen was Speer's idea. In fact, this was only discovered some decades after the war because Speer had long maintained the lie that he knew nothing about the concentration camps — and German historiography helped him. In your fictionalised narrative, Speer clearly seeks to be perceived as the Nazi who is willing to confess his crimes, but he is being performed exactly as the professional liar Wiesenthal suspects him to be and does not reveal what he knows. This creates a strong tension between the unspoken and the sayable, a tension that is found in the latently sadomasochistic relationship between the two.

DG     From the letters, it would appear as if Wiesenthal wanted to believe that Speer was sincere in his regrets and was looking for forgiveness. It is a very interesting quest to forgive your perpetrator.

SB     At the same time, one has the impression that the two men are avoiding a shared truth: Processing and reconditioning after the war manifests in a hopeless labyrinth of allusions and displacements. How is forgiveness possible under this condition? And is this your perspective on the actionable condition of forgiveness?

DG     We will never know their true motivations, but I do believe that part of it was a genuine quest for forgiveness. Even if it seems hopeless, for me it is more interesting to look at this case study as a way to contemplate the present and the future through the past. It is not only about forgiving the other but also forgiving the self, whether it is Speer committing crimes against humanity or Wiesenthal suffering from survivor's guilt. Of course, there is also a lot of self-interest involved. The two protagonists try to use each other for their own legacies. This comes up in the café scene. They are both old and think about how they will be remembered. Wiesenthal offers to help with the difficult parts in Speer's book draft. From his side, Speer offers to talk positively about Wiesenthal to his publisher. They help each other in a way that crosses normative boundaries of victim-perpetrator.

SB     I read this scene as an expression of co-dependence. Speer literally washes his hands, adorned with the innocence of a person who takes credit for the admission of guilt, and in Wiesenthal's case, the viewer can see that he struggles to survive in his own memories. For me, the inevitable failure of their conversation is the most provoking challenge for the idea of forgiveness.

DG     I think that the act of conversation, especially the act of listening, is integral to the process of reconciliation itself.

Albert Speer
dipl. ing.

Heidelberg 1. 11. 1974

Sehr geehrter Herr Wiesenthal,

aller Voraussicht nach ist dieser furchtbare Ausdruck
"Endlösung" eine eindeutige Tarnbezeichnung gewesen.
Auch in meinem Arbeitsbereich gab es zahlreiche
Code-Namen, deren Bedeutung denen, die damit zu tun
hatten, klar war, beispielsweise V-Waffen für die
Peenemünder Raketen. Jedoch hat Hitler nach meiner
Erinnerung nie dieses Wort gebraucht. Er sprach von
der Vernichtung der Juden, von der Rache an den Juden,
wie ich in meinem Nürnberger Tagebuch vermerkt habe.

Auch habe ich mir nochmals die Rede Himmlers vor den
Gauleitern vom 6. Oktober 1943 (bei der ich nicht
anwesend war) durchgelesen. Auch Himmler benutzt
Worte wie ausrotten, umbringen, verschwinden lassen,
aber das Wort Endlösung hat er nicht gebraucht. Mir
selbst ist erinnerlich, dass ich dieser Wortbildung
das erstemal im Nürnberger Prozess begegnet bin.

Das bedeutet aber keineswegs, dass dieser Ausdruck
denjenigen, die im "Sonderreferat Juden" arbeiteten,
nicht geläufig gewesen sein kann.

Jeder Sachverständige wird das bestätigen können.
Und sicher wird in diesem Fall nur durch gutacht-
liche Äusserungen in Ihrem Rechtsstreit Genugtuung
gegeben werden können.

Es tut mir leid, dass ich Ihnen keine bessere Antwort
geben kann. Vielleicht darf ich noch hinzufügen, dass
es mich gefreut hat, von Ihnen einen Brief zu erhalten
und dass nur meine Sorge, aufdringlich zu erscheinen,
mich davon abgehalten hat, Ihnen nach der Lektüre

A letter from Albert Speer to Simon Wiesenthal, 1974

"In all likelihood, the horrible term 'Final Solution' was an explicit code. In my field of operation there were numerous code names whose meanings were clear to those who were involved, such as the case of the retaliatory weapons for the Peenemünde missiles. As far as I can remember, Hitler never used this phrase. He spoke of annihilation of the Jews and revenge on the Jews, as I noted in my Nuremberg Diary. I have additionally re-read through the speech Himmler gave to the Regional Party Leaders from 6 October 1943, where I wasn't present. Himmler used words such as 'eradicating', 'disposing of' and 'killing', but not the term 'Final Solution'. I myself can remember first hearing this term at the Nuremberg trials. However, this does not mean that this expression would not have been familiar to those who worked in the Special Unit for Jews. Any expert would be able to confirm this. And certainly, in this case, you will only be content with expert statements for your legal dispute. I apologise for not being able to provide you with a better answer. Perhaps I may add that I was pleased to receive a letter from you and that it was only my concern about appearing pushy that prevented me from telling you after reading [...]"

The Final Solution. No. I only heard this term after the war.

Dani Gal, *As from Afar*, 2013, film still, camera: Emre Erkmen

Dani Gal, *As from Afar*, 2013, film still, camera: Emre Erkmen

Liliana Cavani, *The Night Porter*, 1974, film still

SB   Aren't they abusing each other, too? But more crucially, truth, in addition to lies and repression, malingers between them and in the way they talk to each other. Does this ethics of mutual and conflictual affection underlying your cinematic concept as such also apply to the relationship between the film and the viewer?

DG   It has to do with this idea of "unsettling empathy" coined by the historian Dominick LaCapra.[6] LaCapra rejects and warns against full identification with the victim: If the historian completely identifies with the victim, there is a loss of critical distance, which can also lead to condescension. He also rejects and warns against full objectivity through maintenance of objective critical distance: the bystander position. He proposes a space between these two approaches and explains it as a way "to work out some very delicate, at times tense, relationship between empathy and critical distance".[7] This delicate relationship is something that I am trying to achieve when working with actors and directing a scene but also in the relationship to the audience. I want the audience to move between empathy and critical distance.

SB   Why do only men appear as key figures within your multifaceted reflections on possible shifts in perpetrator-victim relationships?

DG   All three films feature male protagonists; however, I do not show admiration for them. They are not protagonists in the classical way of "heroes" and the resulting identification experienced by viewers. Maintaining this distance allows for a critical view on the power structures of the male protagonists writing history and how they are represented in cinema. There is also an element of collapse in the world of these protagonists. In *Night and Fog*, Michael Goldman-Gilad says that while he was investigating Eichmann's case, he felt as if he was going through the horror of the camps all over again. Later, when he carries the milk jug that functions as an urn, the silence between the police officers reveals their inability to work through their own emotions. In *As from Afar*, the characters are trapped inside of Haus Wittgenstein before ending up caught inside of a miniature model of the building. And in *White City*, when Arthur Ruppin walks in the city that suddenly becomes an Arab village, it is not clear if it is all in his head. This is after he meets with an Aryan race researcher and finds out that they agree with each other on many levels.

SB   Haus Wittgenstein, finished in December 1928, is modernist in the sense that it is made of stone, glass and metal. We already spoke about

6   See Dominick LaCapra, *Writing History, Writing Trauma*, Johns Hopkins University Press, Baltimore, 2014.
7   LaCapra, *Writing History, Writing Trauma*, p. 147.

how your camera transforms its industrial appearance into a prison, which could also be associated with the architecture of concentration camps. The whiteness of Haus Wittgenstein's design corresponds in an uncanny way with the Weißenhofsiedlung (Weissenhof Estate) in Stuttgart, which becomes the setting for your reflection on historical racial theory. Whiteness serves as an obvious reference to the nickname of Tel Aviv, which you use as the title of the third film in your trilogy. The colour white shows manifold and entangled meanings and relations. I read in it a resonance of critical whiteness in the field of postcolonial theories.

DG  Yes, I take the word "white" from the realm of architecture to the discourse of race. For the Nazis, the "white city" belonged to something that is not white in a racial sense but to the architecture in the Levant, which they saw as primitive. The Weißenhofsiedlung was also built around the same time as Haus Wittgestein, in 1927, and they published a postcard to advertise it. Later the Nazis took the same postcard and photo-montaged camels, Bedouins, and Arab merchants to mock it as architecture that belongs to the Levant and not to Germany. The caption says "1940 Stuttgart. Weissenhofsiedlung, Araberdorf" (Arab village). The earliest postmark I found dates to 1932. It is a projection into the future, as if they wanted to say that Germany will be taken over by Arabs eight years later. It is similar to the rhetoric of the AfD (Alternative for Germany) and PEGIDA (Patriotic Europeans Against the Islamisation of the Occident) following the refugee crisis in 2015.

SB  Or think of Thilo Sarrazin. Until his exclusion in July 2020, he was a member of the SPD (Social Democratic Party of Germany) and published his book, *Deutschland schafft sich ab* (*Germany Abolishes Itself*) in 2010, which is three years before the AfD was founded. Sarrazin's discriminatory pamphlet agitates in an Islamophobic manner against Turkish and Arab citizens, claiming that they reproduce far faster than the German population and would already dominate German society. His racist right-wing rhetoric is doubtlessly an expression of white supremacy. Of course, we have to be careful not to assume any linear logics here; nevertheless, your film reminds the viewer of the lack of demarcation between leading Bauhaus architects like Ludwig Mies van der Rohe and Walter Gropius and the Nazi regime. Le Corbusier was also not innocent in this regard. Before we speak about the specific relationship between Arthur Ruppin and Hans F. K. Günther, I would like to ask you about your perspective on the role of modern architecture for and within modern eugenics.

DG  The architecture historian Fabiola López-Durán pointed out the connection between eugenics and architecture in modernity, especially

The impossibility of forgiveness offers itself to thought, in truth, as its sole possibility. Why is forgiveness impossible? Not merely for a thousand psychological reasons, but absolutely impossible?

Simply because what there is to forgive must be, and must remain, unforgivable. If forgiveness is possible, if there is forgiveness, it must forgive the unforgivable — such is the logical aporia. But, in spite of appearances, this is not only a cold and formal contradiction or logical dead end. [...] If one had to forgive only what is forgivable, even excusable, *venial*, as one says, or insignificant, then one would not forgive. One would excuse, forgive, erase, one would not be granting forgiveness. [...] In order to forgive, one must (*il faut*) therefore forgive the unforgivable, but the unforgivable that remains (*demeuré*) unforgivable, the worst of the worst: the unforgivable that resists any process of transformation of me or of the other, that resists any alteration, any historical reconciliation that would change the conditions or the circumstances of the judgement. Whether remorse or repentance, the ulterior purification of the guilty has nothing to do with this. Besides, there is no question of forgiving a guilty one, a subject subject to transformation beyond the fault. Rather, it is a matter of forgiving the fault itself — [...] impossible? If it remains thus impossible, forgiveness must therefore *do the impossible*; it must undergo the test and ordeal of its own impossibility in forgiving the unforgivable. It must therefore undergo the test and ordeal, merge (*se confondre*) with the very test and ordeal of this aporia or paradox: the possibility, if it is possible and if there is such, the possibility of the impossible. And the impossible *of* the possible.

Jacque Derrida, *Acts of Religion*, Routledge, New York, 2002, p. 385–86.

Dani Gal, *White City*, 2018, film still, camera: Itay Marom

Tel Aviv-Jaffa, 35 mm film still, circa 1933–35

Abb. 14. Araberdorf (Weißenhofsiedlung Stuttgart - Schwäb. Kunstverlag, H. Boettcher, Stuttg.)
(Vgl. Schw. H.-B. 1934, Abb. 132)

weise gerichtet war, machte sich auch der damalige Geschäftsführer des württembergischen Werkbundes über das traditionsverbundene Bauen des Heimatschutzes lustig. Aber die Herrlichkeit der Sieger dauerte nicht lange. Es hieß nur zu schnell: „Ach wie bald schwindet Schönheit und Gestalt! Gestern noch auf stolzen Rossen, heute durch die Brust geschossen." – Jetzt macht man sich über die Erzeugnisse der Weißenhofsiedlung lustig (Abb. 14).

Wer zuletzt lacht, lacht am besten!

### Ju dem Farbdruck Bergstädtchen Altensteig im Schwarzwald

An einem steilabfallenden Südabhang auf dem linken Ufer der oberen Nagold erhebt sich das alte Burg- und Bergstädtchen Altensteig, bekrönt von einem massigen mittelalterlichen Schloß (s. Schw. H.-B. 1940, Seite 45) und der stattlichen Kirche. Diese ist aber erst eine spätere Zutat von 1773-75. Unser Bild zeigt noch den geschlossenen Aufbau des alten Städtchens mit seinen stattlichen Fachwerk-giebelhäusern.

Der Maler des Bildes war Karl Weyßer, geboren am 7. September 1833 in Durlach (Baden). Er studierte zunächst am Polytechnikum, dann (unter Descoutres) an der Kunstschule in Karlsruhe, später noch in München. Er hat hauptsächlich in den 70er Jahren des vorigen Jahrhunderts die malerischen Städtchen Südwestdeutschlands durchwandert und ihre Reize in zahlreichen Zeichnungen, mit feinen Federstrichen und leicht mit verdünnter Tusche laviert, festgehalten. So besitzt auch das Landesamt für Denkmalpflege in Stuttgart eine stattliche Sammlung solcher Zeichnungen aus Württemberg, von denen in den Schwäbischen Heimatbüchern verschiedene abgebildet wurden: 1925, Seite 44, Rathaus Mühlheim a. D., S. 46 altes Fachwerkhaus in Gmünd, Seite 47 Schloß Altensteig; 1930, Seite 153, an der Stadtmauer von Möckmühl; 1933, Seite 130, das alte (abgebrannte) Pfründhaus im Kloster Maulbronn; 1939, Seite 31, Straße in Vaihingen a. E., Seite 34 Marktbrunnen in Rottweil a. N.

Als Maler befaßte sich Weyßer vorwiegend mit Architekturdarstellungen und Städteansichten und malte auch Bildnisse. Seine Ölbilder zeichnen sich durch feine Farbstimmung aus und erinnern an die liebenswürdige Art Spitzwegs.                                                              F. Sch.

31

*Schwäbisches Heimatbuch*, 1941

"In 1927, the Work Union Settlement at the Weißenhofsiedlung in Stuttgart was inaugurated with flags and fanfare, and the victory of the New Objectivity was jubilantly announced to the amazed world. On the evening reception that preceded the opening day of the building exhibition, an exhibition that underscored a departure from traditional building values, the then managing director of the Württemberg Werkbund also chose to make fun of the traditional State Security style of building. But the glory of the victors did not last long. It was said all too quickly 'How soon beauty and form shall fade! Yesterday still on proud horses, today shot in the chest!' Now one makes fun of the outcome of the Weißenhof Estate. He who laughs last, laughs loudest!"

Set photography, *White City*, 2018, photo: Klaus Oppermann

Actor Alexander E. Fennon as Arthur Ruppin with Manfred Ulmer in Haus Le Corbusier at the Weissenhofmuseum, Stuttgart, where Ulmer works.

Le Corbusier at his studio in France, 1962,
photo: Wolfgang Kühn

Set photography, *White City*, 2018, photo: Klaus Oppermann

Dani Gal, *White City*, 2018, film still, camera: Itay Marom

in South America. She writes about the way ideas of eugenics affected concepts of architecture in the early twentieth century, the idea of shaping the new human and engineering society through the body and accommodating the body and society in architecture. The houses in the Weißenhofsiedlung are very small inside in comparison to buildings built today but also in comparison to old German homes. There is a strong feeling that the interior is reduced to the minimum size with maximum functionality.

SB    The eugenically imagined space deals with the removal of all supposedly superfluous decorations, the non-functional aspects of daily life and social communication. Remarkably, the encounter between the two protagonists in *White City*, both eugenicists, also speaks its own language.

DG    Before Ruppin leaves Günther's office in the film's main scene, they briefly talk about two interlinked and significant events that happened at the time in relation to Germany, the Jewish world and Palestine. The first is the anti-Nazi boycott, which was started in May 1933 by the newly founded American League for the Defence of Jewish Rights. The second is the Haavara (transfer) Agreement. In August 1933 — the same month Ruppin visited Günter — the Nazi government and the Jewish Agency signed an agreement that enabled to about 60,000 German Jews to flee Nazi prosecution by emigrating to Palestine and move some of their as-

I'm curious about how you wish
to further refine your people.

Dani Gal, *White City*, 2018, film still, camera: Itay Marom

sets in a form of exported German manufactured goods. The agreement served both the Zionist leaders in Germany and the new Nazi government who tried to get rid of the Jewish population before the Endlösung (Final Solution) existed as a policy. It also negated the efficacy of the anti-Nazi boycott, which started one month after the anti-Jewish boycott.

SB    What is Ruppin's special importance, and what is his relationship to architecture?

DG    Ruppin was a German-Jewish sociologist and one of the founding fathers of Zionism. He opened the Palästina-Amt (Jewish Agency for Palestine) in Jaffa at the beginning of the twentieth century and started to buy land, plan the first settlements and engineer the first pioneer groups. Ruppin also brought Richard Kauffmann to Palestine. Kaufmann was a German-Jewish architect who introduced modernist architecture to Palestine, and he is perhaps the main architect to popularise the style now associated with the idea of Israeli architecture. Another simulation of the connection between ideology and architecture happens through the set design of the two encounters — Ruppin measuring a young Jewish man and Ruppin visiting Günther — both scenes take place in the same room. We constructed the sets so that they mirror each other with a change of light and slightly different props. It is meant to function as a déjà vu when the same room appears ten minutes later in the film edit.

the world Jewry is calling for
a boycott on Germany?

Dani Gal, *White City*, 2018, film still, camera: Itay Marom

A pile of protest signs from an anti-Nazi boycott in the United States lie on the ground, 1933,
photo: Peter Gessner

Also, we're working on a contract for
the conditions of the Transfer Agreement.

Dani Gal, *White City*, 2018, film still, camera: Itay Marom

SB    This mirror effect is reminiscent of the relationship between Wiesenthal and Speer in *As from Afar*. I would like to ask you whether and how you think about the comparison of Günther and Ruppin in relation to your idea of multidirectional memory, empathy and forgiveness? What does the realisation of the eugenic implications of Zionism mean for the victims of the Nazis? I remember your reference to Primo Levi's thought that Nazi ideology was infiltrating the entire spiritual climate.

DG    You mean that Nazi ideology corrupted its victims too? Ruppin had these ideas before the Jewish people became the victims of the Nazis. I think that it had more to do with nationalism, with the fact that the nation state cannot tolerate the other, the foreigner, while simultaneously needing the other in order to define its borders — all borders, not only the geographical ones. The Nazis took this idea to the maximum, to the extreme. Ideas of eugenics and bio-nationalism were popular at the time.

SB    Absolutely, no doubt about that. The Nazis loved Günther for his idea of a biological nationalism. What makes your film so revealing is the realisation that they adopt ideas of a Zionist and thus cannot claim originality. Nonetheless, the analogy shudders.

DG    Everything that Ruppin says in the film is taken from his own writings. Ideas about creating racial hierarchies within the Jewish people —

Set photography, *As from Afar*, 2013, photo: Dani Gal

hierarchies with direct applications during the creation of Israeli society — were ideas that mirror nineteenth-century colonialist exploitation based on categories of racial superiority. For Ruppin, the European Jews were at the top of the hierarchy. For example, the Yemenite Jews were black, and he promoted their immigration as land workers, although back in Yemen they worked as jewellers. The Ethiopian Jews were not even considered Jewish in his view. These hierarchies continue to have implications for Israeli society to this day.

SB    The idea of a biologically coherent population as a basis for a nation state is, as Benedict Anderson would say, an "imagined political community", based on local language communities and universalist concepts of the state as well as on racist hierarchies, which are all respectively discriminatory mechanisms of in- and exclusion. *White City* puts these mechanisms in an explicit colonialist perspective vis-à-vis the constitution of Israel.

DG    Let's think about the amount of destruction that was done in the Nakba with the elimination of over four hundred localities and urban areas, the expulsion of over 700,000 Palestinians, massacres and looting. It is the complete elimination of a culture in the name of progress and the modernist project.

At first glance it might seem strange that the attitude of the anti-Semite can be equated with that of the negro-phobe. It was my philosophy teacher from the Antilles who reminded me one day: "When you hear someone insulting the Jews, pay attention; he is talking about you." And I believed at the time he was universally right, meaning that I was responsible in my body and soul for the fate reserved or my brother. Since then, I have understood that what he meant quite simply was that the anti-Semite is inevitably a negrophobe.

Frantz Fanon, *Black Skin, White Masks* [1952], trans. Richard Philcox, Grove Press, New York, 2008, p. 101.

SB   Of course, this is a crucial historical issue. At the same time, modernism was rejected by the Nazis as an expression of degeneration. As you have mentioned earlier, they sought to destroy the Weißenhofsiedlung because of its resemblance to an "Arab" village.

DG   The Nazis even built a few Germanic style houses in response. When you visit the area, there are a few houses nearby that look almost ridiculously Germanic.

SB   This eclecticism also sheds a significant light on the relationship between Ruppin and Günther: As if they were combining their ideas that deal with the superiority of their own and the inferiority of the "other" — an aspect that is informed by their encounter and interaction. Is this an interpretation your film suggests?

DG   At the time, Günther was the leading figure in the field of race research. For Ruppin, it was almost a side occupation. I wanted to emphasise this dynamic between the two when Ruppin is looking up to a younger scientist and asks for his approval. Again, the idea of the mirror is both formally and conceptually performed in the film. In the first scene, Ruppin is conducting a eugenic test on a young Jewish man...

SB   Who is played by a Palestinian actor...

DG   Yes, by Yousef Sweid, who is Palestinian-Israeli. In mainstream American cinema and television, Israelis often play Arabs, usually terrorists. We rarely see the opposite. I knew Yousef from before and talked to him about it. As an indigenous person, the feeling of being a foreigner in his own country was very familiar. This worked well with the phrase repeated by his character and by Ruppin: "Alles ist Fremd" (Everything is foreign). I also wanted to play with the self-referential idea that the foreigner, Ruppin, is trying to convince the indigenous man to emigrate to his own land and the latter is not interested.

SB   His character also questions Ruppin's idealist pioneering spirit when he mentions that many people committed suicide.

DG   In Israeli schools, we are taught that the first waves of emigration pioneers participated in a positive time of nation building. It was actually very hard and some did not survive this period with the harsh climate and rugged terrain. It was also very hard to be accepted to these groups.

Set photography, *White City*, 2018, photo: Klaus Oppermann

Dani Gal, *White City*, 2018, film stills, camera: Itay Marom

SB    Then there is the actual *Spiegelreflexkamera* (mirror reflex camera), which actualises the mirror effect running through *White City* as a structural medium and procedure.

DG    In addition to the camera, the scene with the young Jewish man ends when he leaves and we see him through the mirror. When Günther enters the room we also see him through the mirror. In addition, there is the eyeball imagery and the reduction of people to the biological, which amplifies this visual thematic.

SB    The collection of eyes reminds me of *Der Sandmann*, a romantic literary narrative by E. T. A. Hoffmann from 1816 that refers to the tension between pre-modern alchemy and modern optical technology. The narrative style is characterised by advanced and uncanny perspectivism. In my opinion, this moment also appears in your film. I see a parallel to the extreme perspectives reminiscent of Bauhaus photography, which are burned into the cultural memory and in which the so-called Arab village is captured in your film.

DG    Just to add to what you are saying, there is also the first Daimler commercial I re-enacted in the film, where we see a model getting out of a car with Le Corbusier's house in the background. Daimler-Benz AG was established in Stuttgart in 1926, a year before the construction of the Weißenhofsiedlung. Using the new architecture for a branding campaign was a way to relate their car to progress.

SB    The young modern woman representing attributes of the upper bourgeois class is a classical symbol of the Weimarer Republik. We see her prototype in your film both as an emancipated, mobile subject and as advertising object for an upscale lifestyle. The myth of Bauhaus as a democratic aesthetic for the masses was already over by this point. Your film is characterised by a stark contrast between the image of luminous, commercial, feminised modernity and the obscure chamber à la Dr Frankenstein in which the two men meet.

DG    Yes, Gothic horror movies: the slices of brain tissue, the eye balls... verses a bright sunny day.

SB    The basics of modernity — invention, progress and enlightenment — seem already contaminated and connected to the dark, proto-fascistic posture of modern times. Does this apprehension correspond to the concerns of *White City*, and perhaps also to the first two films in your trilogy?

DG   I use horror film tropes throughout the trilogy. In *As from Afar*, I plant objects in the model builder's studio: a raven, a piece of a skull, a jaw made of plaster, little Nazi sculptures, a gun. We already mentioned the pieces of brain tissue, the artificial eyes and other images of death in *White City*. When Günther explains his skull chart, he also accidentally brushes his cigarette against it. In *Night and Fog*, there is the foreboding presence of a milk jug full of human ashes.

SB   I am thinking right now about Sylvie Lindeperg's book *"Nuit et brouillard": Un film dans l'histoire* (*"Night and Fog": A Film in History*) published in 2011 about Alain Resnais's film from 1956, especially the chapters in which she writes about the role of Olga Wormser, the historian whose research was so important for the French film director. Since the Nazis had considerable success in erasing and destroying all signs of death they left behind, every object and document found after the war became intensely meaningful for the reconstruction of what had happened. I am thinking of it because this could be a meaningful layer to ponder upon: What objects do we have that are able to really speak in relation to such a gigantic machinery of death?

DG   Your question brings us back to the beginning of the interview about my film *Night and Fog*, which I named after Alain Resnais's film. We talked about Godard's statement of a missing link in the representation and Lanzmann's statement about wanting to destroy any possible evidence. This makes me think of the Israeli government's decision to get rid any trace of Adolf Eichmann so there will be no memorial or place of remembrance for him. But Eichmann is everything but forgotten. One does not need a physical trace or a monument to remember. Growing up in Jerusalem, I lived around many physical traces of Palestinian houses and villages, yet, I never questioned the historical background of these building until I was older. It was not part of my cultural memory because the state didn't want it to be.

SB   This thought could be related to Georges Bataille's critique of modern culture, which includes its dark side, its negativity, and which represents the opposite of the exclusion of death from modern ideas of life as embodied in the vitalism of the life reform movement, not least in the context of Bauhaus. With Michel Foucault we could read this as a manifestation of modern biopower, which of course also relates to modern eugenics. These contexts confront us with the violent and deadly exclusion of death in the name of life based on ideas of healthy, strong and hygienic bodies — "illness" and "dirt" had to be eliminated. Does it make sense to you to relate the imagery and narratives of your films to such topics?

Dani Gal, *White City*, 2018, film still, camera: Itay Marom

Daimler-Benz commercial photographed in front
of Haus Le Corbusier in Stuttgart's
Weißenhofsiedlung, 1928

Dani Gal, *White City*, 2018, film still, camera: Itay Marom

DG    The films are trying to provoke a discussion about forgiveness and it is necessary to arrive at an understanding of forgiveness through multidirectional memory. Humans are capable of extreme violence under certain political conditions and understanding this is a step toward responsibility and away from guilt.

SB    Every crime in the name of a nation state or in the name of an ideology is to be seen in its specific condition, which does not mean that it is not based on overarching developments and structures. One last question regarding the relationship between the specific role of cinematic memory for your approach of forgiveness in the "real" world…

DG    Cinematic memory is always a representation of the event. The boundaries between what we understand the event to be and the representation of it by other means — artistic or documentary — is completely blurred.

SB    There is a pedagogical moment in all of your films, a certain way of teaching us about history. Thinking of Resnais's *Nuit et brouillard*, my question is whether you, as an artist, understand film as a privileged medium of education, of learning or relearning?

DG    What do you mean by relearning? Or do you mean unlearning?

SB   This was the name of the programme that the allies imposed on the Germans and Austrians after the Second World War in order to educate them in democratic educational work. The field of culture — literature, film, visual arts and music — played an important role for the programme. I don't suggest that your trilogy directly refers to this historical project. Nevertheless, the style and atmosphere of your films reminds me of a certain West German television aesthetic that is shaped by the idea of mass education.

DG   I use classic cinema and television tropes in the way of shooting, dramatisation and creating atmospheres. By doing this, the scenes look familiar to the viewer in the sense that you mentioned, yet because the syntax is different, the familiar becomes unfamiliar. In *White City*, through showing the postcards at the beginning and reconstructing them cinematically at the end of the film, I tried to concentrate the entire Palestinian/Israeli/German historical complexity into one image. The "white city" mutates from the untouched postcard of the modern architecture, through the orientalist mockery created by the Nazis, which ironically resembled the reality of pre-1948 Palestine, before bridging into contemporary German Islamophobia, then posing as the naive construction of the "white city" in Israel that was created at the expense of the expulsion of Palestinians and the destruction of their cities and villages.

SB   The picture is obviously very topical if we consider today's forms of Islamophobia. It also reminds me of Beatriz Colomina's book *Privacy and Publicity: Modern Architecture as Mass Media*, in which the architectural theorist examines the dialectics of architecture, postcards and film strips. As such the scene appears as a complex thought-picture, to speak with Walter Benjamin — a montage of fragmented or asynchronous memory that overlaps with the present.

DG   One of these moments happens in *Night and Fog*, when Goldman-Gilad describes how he went home, took his car, drove to the prison, and while walking along the prison walls, he is reminded of Auschwitz, but this time, Goldman-Gilad says, it was "His [Eichmann's] Auschwitz". This aural retelling is overlayed with the scene of the boat carrying Eichmann's ashes taking off into the sea.

SB   During the course of my research on your trilogy, I found texts recounting the delegitimisation of testimonies delivered by the victims of the Shoah. Judges claimed they were too influenced by their affects as a result of their experiences. As much as your films focus on the ethical motive of forgiveness, as much they confront us with personal memories that illustrate the difficulties and hurdles of this claim, your aesthetic and narrative treatments of perpetrator-victim relationships do not allow a solution to this problem but give us the opportunity to address it.

Thus, even if the Holocaust and the Nakba are incomparable events of different magnitude, in other senses they structurally and albeit partially share the same type of dangerous political rationale, together with many other historical phenomena. We underscore the "partially" since neither the Holocaust nor the Nakba, nor the other events to which we have alluded, can be entirely reduced to this political logic alone. Yet this historical and political context, however unsatisfactory, is certainly important and essential to understanding these events. The refugee is therefore a major political and cultural figure who, despite all the difference, links the Jewish Holocaust to the Palestinian Nakba and stands as a figure of radical critique of the exclusionary ethnic model of the nation-state.

Bashir Bashir and Amos Goldberg, "Deliberating the Holocaust and the Nakba: disruptive empathy and binationalism in Israel/Palestine", *Journal of Genocide Research* 16, no. 1, 2014, p. 77–99, here p. 92.

In a sense, there are two extreme possibilities for the historian: the first is the extreme of full identification with participants. In a case such as that of the Holocaust, the figures with whom the historian has identified have generally been bystanders, because the identification with the bystander is closest to the other possibility for the historian — that is, the idea of full objectivity, neutrality, not being a player, not being a participant. But there's also the possibility that the historian (or any other observer), might go to the extreme of full identification, that there is something in the experience of the victim that has almost a compulsive power and should elicit our empathy. This empathy may go to the point of a kind of extreme identification, wherein one becomes a kind of surrogate victim oneself. [...] The alternative to this is trying to work out some very delicate relationship between empathy and critical distance. This is very much the problem of trying to relate acting-out to working-through itself: In acting-out, one relives as if one were the other, including oneself as another in the past; and in working-through, one tries to acquire some critical distance that allows one to engage in life in the present, to assume responsibility — but that doesn't mean that you utterly transcend the past. [...]

I think the binary opposition is very closely related to the scapegoat mechanism, and that part of the process of scapegoating is trying to generate pure binary oppositions between self and other, so that the other (let's say in the context of the Holocaust, the Jew, or the other victim of Nazi oppression), becomes totally different from the Nazi, and everything that causes anxiety in the Nazi is projected onto the other, so you have a pure divide: Aryan/ Jew — absolutely nothing in common. And then you can show that this extreme binarization is actually a way of concealing anxiety, and the ways in which the seemingly pure opposites also share certain things. [...] Acting-out and working-through, in this sense, are a distinction, in that one may never be totally separate from the other, and the two may always be implicated in each other. But it's very important to see them as countervailing forces, and to recognize that there are possibilities of working-through that do not go to the extreme of total transcendence of acting-out, or total transcendence of the past.

Dominick LaCapra, interviewed by Amos Goldberg on 9 June 1998, Yad Vashem, Shoah Resource Center, Jerusalem, p. 3–6.

# HISTORY IN MOTION AND THE PRESENCE OF THE UNTOLD
Burcu Dogramaci

History, as Michel de Certeau explains in his book *The Writing of History*, is written out of contemporary conditions of possibility and production and is thus not objective "fact".[1] Walter Benjamin puts it similarly in *On the Concept of History* (*Über den Begriff der Geschichte*): "History is the object of a construct whose site is not homogenous, empty time, but time filled by Now-Time (*Jetztzeit*)."[2] History is a reformulation of what has occurred, which always carries a degree of deviation within itself: the truth of history does not always remain the same.[3] Historiography is both selective and relational[4] since it arises from the relation of the recipients to their sources or to the events they have experienced. At the same time, historiography serves the situatedness — including the ideological situatedness — and self-assurance of individuals, groups or larger units up to and including the legitimation of nations.[5]

In recent years, the dominance of grand conceptions of history has been increasingly questioned by critical historiography.

1 Michel de Certeau, *The Writing of History*, trans. Tom Conley, Columbia University Press, New York, 1988, p. 10f.
2 Walter Benjamin, *Illuminations*, ed. Hannah Arendt, trans. Harry Zohn, Fontana, London, 1973, p. 263. German original in Walter Benjamin, "Über den Begriff der Geschichte", in *Gesammelte Schriften*, vol. I/2, ed. Hermann Schweppenhäuser and Rolf Tiedemann, Suhrkamp, Frankfurt am Main, 1991, p. 690–708.
3 Reinhart Koselleck, *Zeitschichten: Studien zur Historik*, Suhrkamp, Frankfurt am Main, 2000, p. 294.
4 Lukas Pokorny, *Das Schreiben von Geschichte: Epistemologische Reflexionen*, LIT, Munich, 2011, p. 65ff.
5 Dieter Langewiesche, *Nation, Nationalismus, Nationalstaat in Deutschland und Europa*, Beck, Munich, 2000, p. 25.

Interdisciplinarity, feminist research, and postcolonial and postmigrant perspectives in particular have had a significant impact on the revision of exclusionary historiographies. There has been an increasing demand for absent and marginalised voices to be considered, and as a result, the often singular "truth" of canonical historiography has been challenged. The omission of migrant perspectives from the history of the Federal Republic of Germany, for example, has been criticised.[6] The present text posits that the critique of exclusionary historiography cannot concentrate only on the marginalised exponents of history alone. A critical historiography sets in perspective the overlooked or unheard events of a period in which recognised or well-known protagonists were also involved. The terms "overlooked" and "marginalised" do not refer to the protagonists but to the untold moments themselves. Marginalised history is thus constituted of narratives and events that had been previously eliminated or deliberately overlooked.

Dani Gal's film trilogy *Night and Fog* (2011), *As from Afar* (2013) and *White City* (2018) negotiates the orders of history and the memories attached to it. Gal pulls into visibility the little-noticed or deliberately repressed; moreover, he adds the fictional to the factual while also giving presence to the unwitnessed. This adds the possibility for many other episodes to emerge from within the powerful "grand narrative".[7] Based on a close reading of Gal's trilogy, my contribution formulates the thesis that history is a net full of holes, consisting primarily of the unwritten and the undescribed. It is precisely the cinematic fictionalisation that produces the visible and the material (film, data) that challenges the orders of tradition: What if this history, and not the widely accepted one, was the basis for our collective knowledge? Is not history always "made"? And who decides what is worth remembering?

The trilogy reflects historiography as something that is constructed and formed of omissions, of repressed or unprocessed things. The films also visually demonstrate the ingredients of historiography: oral and written tradition; visual, acoustical and textual memory; recording by the media and the interpretation of the record. Gal queries the interplay and power relations between these different formats of historiography. His films question the memory shared between source-based cinematic and fictional re-enactments, allowing us to start again from the necessary assumption that history is made and done.

6    See for example Manuela Bojadžijev and Regina Römhild, "Was kommt nach dem 'transnational turn'? Perspektiven für eine kritische Migrationsforschung", in *Vom Rand ins Zentrum: Perspektiven einer kritischen Migrationsforschung*, Panama Verlag, Berlin, 2014, p. 10–24.
7    The term is introduced in Jean-François Lyotard, *The Postmodern Condition*, trans. Geoff Bennington and Brian Massumi, Manchester University Press, Manchester, 1979.

# *NIGHT AND FOG*:
## THE MAKING OF HISTORIOGRAPHY

What colour does history have? And what images does history produce? The opening scene of *Night and Fog* draws the viewer into an overhead shot of a furnace emitting white smoke by night, a visual effect that significantly desaturates the colour palette on the screen. This pallid vision accentuates the scene's affinity to black-and-white cinematography. It is not until the main cast is named that the colour schema appears to enrich in density. *Night and Fog* is devoted to two historical antagonists who are entangled in a peculiar relationship. Adolf Eichmann, head of the Judenreferat (Jewish Section) of the Reichssicherheitshauptamt (Reich Main Security Office) from the end of 1938 and responsible for the "final solution" of the "Jewish question", is sentenced to death in Israel and subsequently cremated. His ashes are to be scattered in the sea off the coast of Jaffa directly after the cremation, during the night of 31 May to 1 June 1962. This task is undertaken by a small group of policemen who, standing around the furnace of the crematorium, stare at the ashes of the National Socialist perpetrator before sweeping them into a milk can. There is to be no territorial memorial site for Eichmann and the ashes are dispersed in the sea. Two policemen, accompanied by a cleric, board a motorboat and carry out the task. One of the two policemen was Michael Goldman-Gilad, himself a Holocaust survivor and Israeli of Polish origin. The narrator's voice-over and the cinematic portrayal of this night are based on his memories and a conversation between Goldman-Gilad and the artist.

The soundtrack itself offers insight, independently of the imagery. There is little talk; the men are sure of their mission, the onus of the operation and the verdict of secrecy. The actions seem well-practiced. The noises of the furnace, the echoing footsteps of the policemen in the corridor, the sound of the bus in which the group rides to the harbour, the engine of the boat and finally the sound of the sea are crucial for the structure of the story. Further amplification comes from the sonorous voice of the narrator, transmitted with interruptions, describing what is taking place, providing annotations to the telling his own story. As Goldman-Gilad walks through the prison to the crematorium, he says: "While walking along the prison walls I thought, this is like Auschwitz, only this time it is his Auschwitz". Gal thus links three chronological levels: that of Auschwitz in the 1940s, that of Ramla Prison in 1962, and that of the present moment when the cinematic images retrieve the story. At the same time his statement reverses the roles of victim and perpetrator. The traumatic experience that is Auschwitz comes to haunt the National Socialist perpetrator, the hangman becomes the hanged man,

Dani Gal, *Night and Fog*, 2011, film stills, camera: Itay Marom

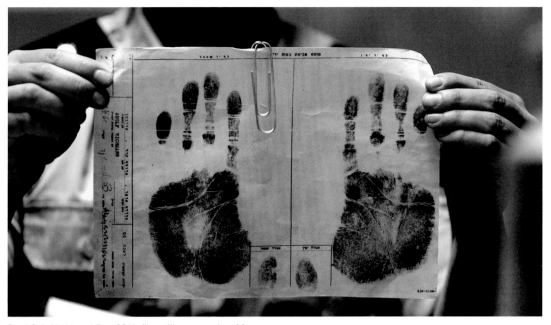

Dani Gal, *Night and Fog*, 2011, film still, camera: Itay Marom

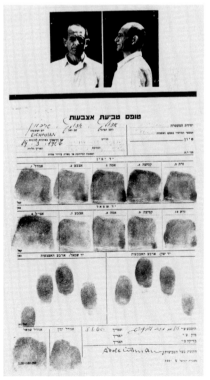

Police officer Michael Goldman-Gilad,
witness at the Eichmann trial, Jerusalem, 1961

Adolf Eichmann's fingerprints
on an Israeli Police document, 1961

Dani Gal, *Night and Fog*, 2011, film still, camera: Itay Marom

Boxes and milk jugs found buried in the ruins of the Warsaw Ghetto,
Poland, that were used to conceal and preserve documents later collected
in the Ringelblum "Oneg Shabat" Archive

with Goldman-Gilad inevitably switching into the role of the participants who carry out the task.

The soundscape is space-forming and narrative. The movements of the silent actors appear to be calm — almost as assured as those of sleepwalkers — and their actions are momentously communicated in the measured slow choreography enacted across an illuminated darkness to great effect. The camera possesses an auctorial instance. It enables intimate scenes, observes the prison from a bird's-eye perspective, or remains outside when the doors of the transport bus close. As for the colour of the images, they too create historical brackets. In the text of the opening slide of his film, Gal describes the appearances of the contemporary witnesses during the Eichmann trial, who are given ample space to recount their traumatic experiences and the violence in the camps. In the report on the Eichmann trial by the Dutch writer Harry Mulisch, a separate chapter is devoted to the testimonies by witnesses.[8] Part of the time allocated to their accounts takes place during a screening of the 1956 film *Nuit et brouillard* (*Night and Fog*) by Alain Resnais. The film was projected without sound, and the soundtrack was replaced by the voices of Shoah survivors who were in attendance. The opening slide of Gal's *Night and Fog* evokes an effect of black-and-white cinema and can be read as an aesthetic reference to this historical courtroom situation.[9] Moreover, the Eichmann trial, which began on 11 April 1961, has been archived in many black-and-white photographs and film reels and only a few colour pictures are in circulation and is critical to how the trial and its defendant are remembered.[10] This brings us to the question as to how black and white and colour impact the representation of history.[11]

Director Alain Resnais comments: "In memory you tend to think in grey or at any rate in a colour that is less clear."[12] With its footage alternating between colour and desaturation, Gal's *Night and Fog* makes a clear reference to Resnais's *Nuit et brouillard* — and not only in its title. *Nuit et brouillard* is constructed out of black-and-white documentary and archive material from concentration camps after their liberation by the Allies. In addition to the found footage, during a subsequent visit

8  Harry Mulisch, *Strafsache 40/61: Eine Reportage über den Eichmann-Prozeß* [1963], Aufbau, Berlin, 1996, see the chapter "Der Greuel und sein Bild", p. 121–29.

9  See Noit Banai and Sabeth Buchmann, "Cinema with/in History: Techniques of Affect, Strategies of Mediality, and Processes of Multidirectional Memory in Contemporary Art", *Texte zur Kunst*, no. 119, September 2020, p. 120–43.

10  See the exhibition *Der Prozess – Adolf Eichmann vor Gericht* (*Facing Justice – Adolf Eichmann on Trial*), Stiftung Topographie des Terrors, Berlin, 2011.

11  On the primacy of black and white in the media transmission of historical material, see Peter Geimer, "Die Farben der Geschichte und die 'Wahrheit des Schwarz-Weiß'", in *Schwarz/Weiß als Evidenz: "With black and white you can keep more of a distance"*, ed. Monika Wagner and Helmut Lethen, Campus, Frankfurt am Main, 2015, p. 246–58.

12  Alain Resnais (1961), quotation by Peter W. Jansen, "Kommentierte Filmografie", in *Reihe Film 38: Alain Resnais*, Carl Hanser, Munich, 1990, p. 63–242, here p. 78.

to Auschwitz-Birkenau, Resnais shot the abandoned and dilapidated camp in colour film. These colour photographs are underlaid with a recorded text by the resistance fighter, writer and concentration camp survivor Jean Cayrol.[13] Thus, another way *Night and Fog* takes its conceptual bearings from *Nuit et brouillard* is in having a voice-over over colour film. The translation for the German version of *Nuit et brouillard* was done by Paul Celan. In their analysis, Noit Banai and Sabeth Buchmann point out the presumed multidirectional references in Gal's *Night and Fog*, recognising in the dark sea a reference to Celan's poem "Todesfuge"[14] (Fugue of Death) with the repeating line "Schwarze Milch der Frühe" (Black milk of dawn) and the milk can that makes an allusion to the container in which a camera was once smuggled into Auschwitz-Birkenau.[15] Above and beyond these possible forms of reference, *Night and Fog* is a secret story materialised in moving images. Based on the story of a witness, time and space become retrospectively fused. Here, in the liminal condition of this recounting, something that is not meant to be remembered becomes very concrete. Told here are a few hours from the continuum of history that were not meant to be recalled.

However, *Night and Fog* can also be read as a reflection that has been turned into a film about how historiography functions. Every event passed down and recorded in writing is composed of various elements: a date, the interaction of persons in specific locations that leads to momentous results. Actions, conversations, noises and even smells constitute the event, but it is only remembered once its significance has been understood and once records, most commonly textual or graphic, exist. In *Night and Fog*, the source and the witness of the event, Michael Goldman-Gilad, is heard as a voice-over, while the moving images and sound develop an inherent logic of their own. Yet the film does not purport to be a document. The leading protagonists and their actors are clearly named as the cast launches into the first scene in the office. This obvious re-enactment of an event manifested by oral tradition emphasises the fact that all historiography is a re-telling of some kind. At the same time, films like Gal's *Night and Fog*, even while admitting to being a fictionalisation in retrospect, can serve — again in the sense of a "historiophoty"[16] — as a critical source for historians or a historiological film analysis. This means that *Night and*

13   Jansen, "Kommentierte Filmografie", p. 80.
14   Paul Celan wrote the poem in 1944–45, published it in Romanian in 1947, and in German in 1948.
15   See Banai and Buchmann, "Cinema with/in History".
16   Hayden White defines the term as a representation of history in visual images and filmic discourses in analogy with historiography, which refers to the representation of history in textual sources. Hayden White, "Historiography and Historiophoty", *The American Historical Review* 93, no. 5, 1988, p. 1193–99. See also Martin Gronau, "Der Film als Ort der Geschichts(de)konstruktion: Reflexion zu einer geschichtswissenschaftlichen Filmanalyse", *AEON – Forum für junge Geschichtswissenschaft* 1, 2009, p. 18–39, here p. 19.

*Fog* inevitably becomes part of a historiography, just as Resnais's *Nuit et brouillard* was also used as evidence in the Eichmann trial.


## AS FROM AFAR:
## MODELS OF REALITY

*As from Afar* brings together two figures of contemporary history who are generally perceived as antagonists: the publicist and architect Simon Wiesenthal, who devoted his life to the conviction of Nazi criminals, and the chief architect of the "Third Reich", Albert Speer, who as a National Socialist perpetrator served a lengthy prison sentence and subsequently relativised his complicity in his autobiography, thus admitting his guilt while simultaneously attempting to justify himself.[17] In *As from Afar*, the two men meet in the workshop of Herr Kuck in which a model of the entrance of the Mauthausen concentration camp is being constructed. Their conversation concerns the realistic reconstruction, but their recollections differ. Herr Kuck explains how he designed the model from memory as a backdrop that has been commissioned for an American film production. He has fulfilled their wishes for railway tracks because otherwise it would not look like a "concentration camp". For all its divergence, the architectural model evokes memories of the contemporary witnesses: Wiesenthal himself is reminded of his stay in Mauthausen and the labour in the quarries. Speer, in turn, claims to only remember one visit to Mauthausen in March 1943.

Not long afterwards, the two elderly gentlemen set off on a walk through what seems to be the "Viennese Old Town" that takes them to a café (although it is actually all taking place on a sound stage at the Bavaria Filmstadt). Their conversation is about guilt and repentance but also about the public perception of their autobiographical books, which express their personal perspectives of the events after 1933. The conversation also reveals things that are difficult to hear and digest, such as when Wiesenthal describes his interlocutor as a blameless witness of history despite the fact that Speer was the minister for armament and ammunition since 1942. Shortly after, during an unobserved moment, Wiesenthal pulls from his pocket a newspaper article in which the concentration camp of Mauthausen is shown to have been Speer's initiative. Later in the film, they continue their walk to the house that philosopher Ludwig Wittgenstein designed together with architect Paul Engelmann for Wittgenstein's sister Margaret Stonborough-Wittgenstein in the unembellished aesthetics of the Neues Bauen (New Building) movement. The film ultimately ends in

---

17  Albert Speer, *Erinnerungen*, Ullstein, Frankfurt am Main, 1969.

Dani Gal, *As from Afar*, 2013, film stills, camera: Emre Erkmen

Dani Gal, *As from Afar*, 2013, film stills, camera: Emre Erkmen

Dani Gal, *As from Afar*, 2013, film still, camera: Emre Erkmen

Haus Wittgenstein, Vienna, 1971, photo: Elfriede Mejchar

I'm almost ashamed.

Dani Gal, *As from Afar*, 2013, film still, camera: Emre Erkmen

front of a model of Haus Wittgenstein that is being constructed by Herr Kuck in his workshop.

Wittgenstein's reflections on memory images in his *Brown Book*, first published in 1958, constitute the framework encompassing the encounter between Wiesenthal and Speer. In the form of an acousmatic voice, Wittgenstein's words address the viewer at the very beginning of the film: "What is the difference between a memory image, [...] and the image in a daydream?" These reflections by Wittgenstein touch on the gulf between events that are experienced, remembered and handed down. Memory includes something added, invented, reconstructed, dreamt of. The dialogues between Wiesenthal and Speer demonstrates how far off the mark — and per contra how accurate — reminiscent perspectives on an era can be. In Gal's film the interlocutors sometimes seem to talk past each other and make statements that do not really reach the other person. As a result, there is a theatrical dimension filtering their intimate constellation. Their conversational script for *As from Afar* is based on a letter correspondence between the two men, itself a communication at distance with a time lag.

It was in January 1975 that Speer first got in touch with Wiesenthal. In his biography, historian Tom Segev devoted some attention to Wiesenthal's exchange with Speer and was the first scholar to focus on this impossible relationship.[18] Impossible, because it described the

---

18 Tom Segev, *Simon Wiesenthal: The Life and Legends*, trans. Ronnie Hope, Doubleday, New York, 2010, p. 390–93.

longstanding intimacy between a perpetrator and a victim of the National Socialist regime that was desired and enjoyed by both. Segev tries to explain the "friendship" between Speer, former National Socialist minister of armaments, and Wiesenthal, who helped to ferret out National Socialist perpetrators:

> I can understand why Albert Speer needed Wiesenthal's friendship, because he invested a great deal in his image-building after he was released from Spandau Prison. But why is it that Wiesenthal needed this friendship? —Well, it started with Speer asking him whether he would receive him in his office, and offhand, I would say that was a kind of victory for Wiesenthal as a Holocaust survivor. Here comes Hitler's closest friend asking for his friendship, his company, his acceptance, and that was at first a victory for him as a Holocaust survivor. Then later on, this friendship brought to light the fact that throughout his life, Wiesenthal was burdened with a very deep feeling of guilt. And I believe it is a kind of identification between a victim and the perpetrator.[19]

Yet, how is Segev's analysis related to the connection Wittgenstein sees between remembering and dreaming, which include a large share of imagination? For many years Wiesenthal and Speer wrote to each other, and from this dialogue, which was primarily conducted in writing, Gal distils a walk that leads through the era and the way it is being interpreted. We have here a meeting between two elderly gentlemen who, through their actions and the textualisation of their perspective on things, were writing history. Their books — Speer's memoir reached three million readers and was made into a movie — are building blocks for the reception of the two protagonists while also helping to define the future perception of history. In his book *Albert Speer: Eine deutsche Karriere* (Albert Speer: A German career), Markus Brechtken compares Speer's memoir with historical sources, revealing how there were substantial manipulations that had an impact on the reception of National Socialist history.[20] At the same time, *As from Afar* is not a positioning of a falsified history; rather, it reflects the processes of reconstructing history that are inevitably characterised by shifts, interpretations and deviations.

19   Tom Segev in conversation with Christoph Heinemann, "Er lebte eigentlich von Enttäuschung zu Enttäuschung", *Deutschlandfunk*, October 2010, https://www.deutschlandfunk.de/er-lebte-eigentlich-von-enttaeuschung-zu-enttaeuschung.694.de.html?dram:article_id=69117. Accessed 4 January 2021. Translation from the German by Ilze Mueller.
20   Markus Brechtken, *Albert Speer: Eine deutsche Karriere*, Siedler, Munich, 2017.

The discussion between Speer, Wiesenthal and Herr Kuck in front of the model of Mauthausen makes clear the extent to which perspectives on the same subject can deviate. Generally, history and its historiography in *As from Afar* deals significantly with the concept of the model, which contains an ambiguity. On the one hand, the model in architecture implies the scaled implementation of a building that has not yet been realised; an articulation of the central concepts. In this function, the architectural model refers to the future and is therefore not so much factual reality as simulation or idea. On the other hand, the model can also reconstruct something that already exists (such as the concentration camp of Mauthausen). There is always some discrepancy in this work of reconstruction, which leads to heated debates, especially in the case of architectural reconstructions (for example, the Berliner Schloss or the Bornplatzsynagoge in Hamburg), as history cannot be brought back.[21] Reconstructions are carried out in the present but refer back to what is past, while the architectural model, which is a design concept, points from the present into the future.

In *The Poetics of Space*, phenomenologist Gaston Bachelard describes how living and growing up in buildings leaves traces in our memory. Certain door handles, a creaking stair or the smell of floor polish or of old wood may conjure memories, even if they date back years.[22] At the same time, says Bachelard, it is especially the house of one's parents that is not only a residential building but also "a dream building": "Every one of its nooks and corners was a refuge for dreaming."[23] In other words, Bachelard interweaves immediate experience with bodily memory and dreaming. In the case of Gal's *As from Afar*, Robert Schumann's musical piece "Wie aus der Ferne" ("As from Afar") from the *Davidsbündlertänze* provides the film's title and is played several times. For Wittgenstein, hearing Schumann's piece was an example of reimagining the past. Gal describes it as follows: "Wittgenstein, in the text I used [for the script], takes Robert Schumann's composition for piano […] as an example and an exercise for an expression of the feeling of pastness. This piece […] is played four times throughout the film, each time in a slightly different way."[24]

Separately, Wiesenthal and Speer wander through Haus Wittgenstein as though they wanted to appropriate the rooms and their history while

21  On debates related to the Berliner Schloss see: http://schlossdebatte.de. For the struggles of the reconstruction of the Bornplatz Synagogue in Hamburg see: https://www.zeit.de/2021/03/bornplatzsynagoge-wiederaufbau-streit-erneuerung-judentum. On common debates and critique regarding the reconstruction of architecture see: *arch+* 204, October 2011, https://www.archplus.net/home/archiv/ausgabe/46,202,1,0.html. Accessed 10 January 2021.

22  Gaston Bachelard, *Poetik des Raumes* [1957], trans. Kurt Leonhard, Fischer, Frankfurt am Main, 2007, p. 34.

23  Bachelard, *Poetik des Raumes*, p. 39.

24  Interview, "Dani Gal Discusses *As from Afar* with Jens Hoffmann", Jewish Museum, 5 December 2014, https://stories.thejewishmuseum.org/dani-gal-discusses-as-from-afar-with-jens-hoffmann-6ddba61d78d5. Accessed 11 January 2021.

sleepwalking through them. Earlier in their conversation it is noted in passing that Wittgenstein and Adolf Hitler knew each other personally and were schoolmates in Linz. The reference might conceal yet another missing historical link: the 1998 publication of Kimberley Cornish's controversial book *The Jew of Linz*, which traces back Hitler's anti-Semitism to his meeting — perhaps even a homoerotic relationship — with Wittgenstein at the Linz secondary school.[25] Admittedly Cornish's book did not gain acceptance and was dismissed as unverified and unscholarly. It did not receive renewed attention until ten years later in a complex essay by Tom Appleton, who discussed various aspects of the book critically and came to a realisation: "After the publication of the English edition, the book had already gotten powerfully slated in reviews from German-speaking countries, but I consider it to be so interesting that the total silence with which it has been greeted since the publication of the German edition, seems to me, [to be] a downright recklessly inadmissible way of treating it, a deliberate clinging to a deadlocked optic, a defence of the blind spot — basically a refusal to perceive one's own history in a truly unbiased way."[26] Similarly, *As from Afar* draws attention to a personal correspondence between a National Socialist perpetrator and a "Nazi hunter" that raises many questions.

## *WHITE CITY*: AN INTERSECTION OF CONFLICTING HISTORIES

Another largely ignored constellation between two antagonists during the 1930s is the subject of the third film of the trilogy, *White City*.[27] Gal conflates a number of different storylines and places: the creation of the Weißenhofsiedlung in Stuttgart as a project of the modern movement and the "White City" of Tel Aviv, which is also considered to be "Bauhausian", with its International Style housing developments. Gal also brings in a Zionist pioneer and one of the founders of Tel Aviv, Arthur Ruppin, who was interested in eugenics and his meeting with the National Socialist racial ideologist Hans F. K. Günther. *White City* begins with a postcard that portrays the Weißenhofsiedlung as "Arab" — a defamation by the political right depicting ground traders hawking their wares in front of the modernist architecture with a procession of camels walking past them. A second postcard appears, showing the above-mentioned

25  Kimberley Cornish, *The Jew of Linz: Hitler, Wittgenstein and their secret battle for the mind*, Century, London, 1998.

26  Tom Appleton, "Wittgenstein und Hitler?", *Telepolis*, 22 March 2008, https://www.heise.de/-3417433. Accessed 11 January 2021. Translation from the German by Ilze Mueller.

27  See also the conversation between Dani Gal and Burcu Dogramaci, "Zionism and Modernity in 'White City'", Taking Measures, 2020, on https://takingmeasures.ch. Accessed 17 January 2021.

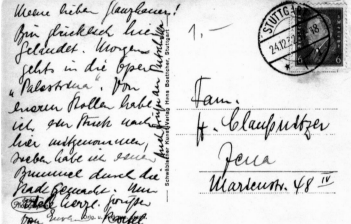

"My dear Glaußhauers!

I have happily landed here. Tomorrow I am going to the opera 'Palestrina'. I brought one piece of your fruitcake and I have just taken a stroll though the city.

Many heartfelt greetings from your Rachel

Fam. H. Glaußnitzer Jena
Marienstr. 48 IV"

"1940 Stuttgart. Weissenhofsiedlung, Araberdorf", postcard, circa 1932

Back side of the original Weißenhofsiedlung postcard that has been photomontaged to look like an "Arab" village; Front side of this same postcard, postmarked 24 December 1932.

and we'll be the lords of the land!

Dani Gal, *White City*, 2018, film stills, camera: Itay Marom

Weißenhofsiedlung as an image without manipulative interventions, as an archetypal housing development of the Neues Bauen movement.

An initial key scene from *White City* shows Arthur Ruppin at work: he measures and photographs a young man. He tries to persuade the young man to "return" to Palestine. Presumably this fictional scene dates back to a time when Ruppin was taking photos for his publications on eugenics. In an essay published in 1918 in the periodical *Der Jude*, Ruppin demands racial hygiene and the "selection of human material" as a condition for a Jewish state that would be established in Palestine.[28] The ideal immigrant should be physically strong, no more than thirty years old and married to a woman who also wants to help with farm work. Ruppin was also head of the Eretz Yisrael Office (a Zionist organisation) and was thus substantially involved in the "pioneering and development phase of pre-state Israel".[29] Before his first Palestine trip in 1907, he was director of the newly established Bureau für Statistik der Juden (Bureau for Jewish statistics and demography) in Berlin. All of this work culminated in the two-volume book *Soziologie der Juden*, published in 1930 by Jüdischer Verlag Berlin, in which Ruppin also addresses the "racial position of the Jews", operating with "racial" concepts such as "inbreeding", "selection" and "blood".[30] Ruppin must have been struck by the parallels to National Socialist racial ideology. His diary contains a passage dated 31 January 1930, written in Jerusalem: "Last week, in a Tel Aviv bookshop, I found a recently published book by Hans F. K. Günther: *Rassenkunde des jüdischen Volkes*. It contains some ideas [paths of thought] and photographs of antique pictures that I would like to include in my book. Fortunately, the race question will take up only a small amount of space in my book."[31]

A few years later in 1933, there was a meeting between Günther, who had published his book *Rassenkunde des deutschen Volkes* in 1922, and Ruppin. "Through Dr Georg Landauer, I travelled to Jena on 11 August to meet Professor Hans F. K. Günther, the founder of National Socialist race theory. The conversation lasted two hours. Günther was most congenial but refused to accept credit for coining the Aryan-concept, and agreed with me that the Jews are not inferior but different, and that the Jewish Question has to be regulated properly."[32] In Gal's film, this short entry becomes a central scene and

28  Arthur Ruppin, "Die Auslese des Menschenmaterials", *Der Jude* 3, no. 8–9, 1918–19, p. 373–83.

29  For more details, see Ita Heinze-Greenberg, *Europa in Palästina: Die Architekten des zionistischen Projekts 1902–1923*, gta Verlag, Zurich, 2011, p. 84. See also Etan Bloom, "The 'Administrative Knight' – Arthur Ruppin and the Rise of Zionist Statistics", in *Tel Aviver Jahrbuch für deutsche Geschichte XXXV (2007): Demographie – Demokratie – Geschichte; Deutschland und Israel*, ed. José Brunner, Wallstein, Göttingen, 2007, p. 183–203.

30  Arthur Ruppin, *Soziologie der Juden*, vol. 1, Jüdischer Verlag, Berlin, 1930, p. 36.

31  Arthur Ruppin, *Tagebücher, Briefe, Erinnerungen*, ed. Schlomo Krolik, Jüdischer Verlag Athenäum, Königstein im Taunus, 1985, p. 422. Translation from the German by Ilze Mueller.

32  Ruppin, *Tagebücher, Briefe, Erinnerungen*, p. 466.

But tell me, what did the [Palestinian] nationalist movement posted in the cities do apart from demonstrate against Jewish immigration?

I'm not saying you weren't right. But in those days, when the Nazi beast was exterminating the Jews of Europe, what did you know about the world?

I'm not saying — no, don't worry. I believe, like you, that this country must belong to its people, and there is no moral, political, humanitarian, or religious justification that would permit the expulsion of an entire people from its country and the transformation of what remained of them into second-class citizens. So, no, don't worry. This Palestine, no matter how many names they give it, will always be Palestinian. But tell me, in the faces of people being driven to slaughter, don't you see something resembling your own?

Don't tell me you didn't know, and above all, don't say that it wasn't our fault.

You and I and every human being on the face of the planet should have known and not stood by in silence, should have prevented that beast from destroying its victims in that barbaric, unprecedented manner. Not because the victims were Jews but because their death meant the death of humanity within us.

Elias Khoury, *Gate of the Sun: Bab al-Shams* [1998], trans. Humphrey Davies, Archipelago Books, Brooklyn, 2006, p. 430–31.

a meeting of two convictions that are diametrically opposed. One is an anti-Semite, the other a Zionist. And yet their methods and biopolitical beliefs are so contiguous that the film offers the paradoxical situation of these two men agreeing on the fact that ethnic and religious origins can be physiognomically quantified. Gal thus hits a nerve: race ideology cannot inevitably be assigned only to Günther[33] but rather equally represents Ruppin's views.

Günther's race ideology aimed in particular at creating the contours of a Nordic "race", as he synoptically linked physical and mental characteristics (which he called the "racial soul") to qualities such as "sagacity, truthfulness and energy".[34] Gal stages the meeting as an intimate dialogue between two antipodes who nevertheless come to develop certain similarities and sympathies.[35] Incidentally, both used photography to support their arguments. Günther employed racist visual imagery and a "visual text"[36] in order to convince his readership. He followed the basic

33  See for example Hans Friedrich Karl Günther, *Rassenkunde des deutschen Volkes* (*Racial Science of the German People*), J. F. Lehmann, Munich, 1926.

34  See Peter Emil Becker, *Sozialdarwinismus, Rassismus, Antisemitismus und Völkischer Gedanke: Wege ins Dritte Reich, Teil II*, Georg Thieme Verlag, Stuttgart, 1990, p. 237.

35  The architecture historian Ita Heintze-Greenberg, too, describes the meeting of 11 August 1933 in a study at the University of Jena as "a two-hour scholarly exchange between two professors that we find disconcerting today". Heinze-Greenberg, *Europa in Palästina*, p. 94.

36  Amos Morris-Reich, *Race and Photography: Racial Photography as Scientific Evidence, 1876–1980*, University of Chicago Press, Chicago, 2016, p. 118.

Dr Arthur Ruppin, circa 1933,
photographer unknown

Prof. Dr Hans F. K. Günther, 1935,
photographer unknown

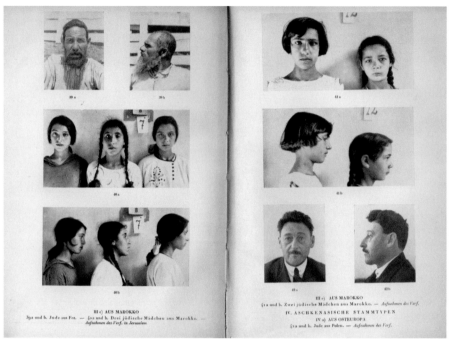

Arthur Ruppin, *Soziologie der Juden*, Jüdischer Verlag, Berlin, 1930

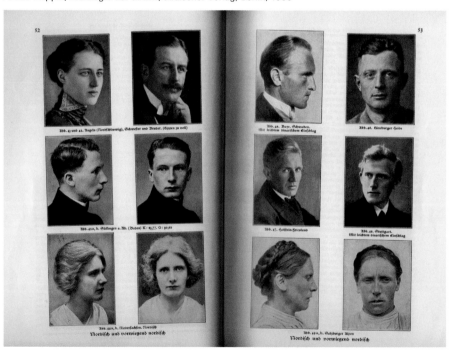

Hans F. K. Günther, *Rassenkunde des deutschen Volkes* [1926], J. F. Lehmann Verlag, Munich, 1933

Dani Gal, *White City*, 2018, film still, camera: Itay Marom

pattern of repetition in order to argue concisely and construct homogeneous types.[37] The photographs on Ruppin's desk in *White City* refer to the presumed photographic practice of Ruppin, who also used photography as a tool for data collection and to illustrate his writings. Among the photographs is a drawing made by architect Richard Kauffmann, a reference to Ruppin's function as head of the Palästina-Amt (Palestine office) and his appointment of Kauffmann at the end of 1920 as the lead architect of the Palestine Land Development Company. Subsequently Kauffmann developed almost 150 moshavim, kibbutzim and garden city-like estates in Palestine, the later Israel. Kauffmann made himself "a name in Israel as the first and foremost estate planner in the country [...]. Some regarded him as 'The City Planner' of the Old New Land par excellence".[38] There is thus a clear link between Ruppin and modernist architecture in Palestine. Kauffmann also designed buildings for Tel Aviv and Haifa.

The film title *White City* refers to Tel Aviv, which has gone down in architecture history as the "White City" of the Neues Bauen in exile. "White" is the outer shell of many buildings, some of which hark back to the plans of emigrated former Bauhaus students or the parameters of Weimar Republic-era modern architecture. "White City" also refers to the Weißenhofsiedlung in Stuttgart. The connection between Ruppin and

37  Morris-Reich, *Race and Photography*, p. 119f.
38  Heinze-Greenberg, *Europa in Palästina*, p. 182.

the Weißenhofsiedlung through which Ruppin strolls, lost in thought, can be made on several levels. Ruppin's own presence in the film directs attention to the debate that was already taking place in the 1920s around the future of German Jewish population outside Germany and in Palestine, which resulted in mass emigration after 1933. Thus, the exile of protagonists (not only to Palestine), as well as the emigration of basic aesthetic principles of the Neues Bauen, was already inscribed in the architecture of the Weißenhofsiedlung. For a long time, it was little known that the building materials for "White City" Tel Aviv and other Jewish settlements also came from Nazi Germany on the basis of an agreement between Zionist organisations and the Reich Ministry of Economics[39] — so one can speak not only of émigré architects but also of migrated materials.

In Sharon Rotbard's book *White City, Black City: Architecture and War in Tel Aviv and Jaffa*, the "Black City" embodies the diametrical opposite or repressed Other of the "White City".[40] Among other places besides Jaffa, the "Black City" designates the Arab quarter called Menashiya, which was destroyed in 1948 and whose inhabitants were driven out. As Rotbard writes, the "Black City" Jaffa was "cleansed" of Arab-Palestinians and "Hebraicised" during the "War of Independence" when Arabic inscriptions were eliminated from daily life.[41] "Black", argues the book, refers to the darker skin colour of Arab-Palestinians, in contrast to the "white" European Jewish population who settled in Palestine in the early twentieth century, and Tel Aviv became a "white city" that was in keeping with the colour of their skin. Although this dichotomous argument about skin colour is certainly problematic in the context of Palestine/Israel and immigration to Israel, Rotbard's book can open up a new uncomfortable perspective on the connotations of "white" architecture. This is where Gal's *White City* connects: In the last scene, the film's protagonist has a vision as he strolls through the Weißenhofsiedlung. The housing colony is transformed into the very scene that was depicted on the defamatory postcard: it turns into an "Arab village".

In the Weißenhofsiedlung Ruppin encounters an imagined problem that continually preoccupied him in his diary entries: the conflict between Arab and Jewish populations.[42] After the bloody riots of 1929 in Hebron, however, a disenchanted Ruppin realised that peaceful coexistence was not possible (yet).[43] Nevertheless, he continued to support the settlement

39  See Ines Sonder and Joachim Trezib, "Baumaterial aus Nazi-Deutsland in Tel Aviv", *Bauwelt*, no. 26, 2019, p. 58–59, https://www.bauwelt.de/26.2019-3303474.html. Accessed 29 January 2021.

40  Sharon Rotbard, *White City, Black City: Architecture and War in Tel Aviv and Jaffa*, Pluto Press, London, 2015.

41  Rotbard, *White City, Black City*, p. 107–14.

42  Arthur Ruppin, diary entry dated 1 June 1936, in Ruppin, *Tagebücher, Briefe, Erinnerungen*, p. 472. See also Alex Bein, "Nachwort: Arthur Ruppin, der Mensch und sein Werk", in Ruppin *Tagebücher, Briefe, Erinnerungen*, p. 547–84, here p. 579.

43  Arthur Ruppin, *Soziologie der Juden*, vol. 2, Jüdischer Verlag Berlin, 1930, p. 296f.

of Palestine, which would involve immigration, the purchasing of land and settlement rights.[44] The film itself ends with images of deportation: the Arab inhabitants of the city are carrying their luggage toward a truck that has just arrived to transport them away. With this imagery, Gal refers back to photographs of the Nakba — the flight and expulsion of roughly 750,000 Arab-Palestinians between 1947 and 1949. Palestine, which since the break-up of the Ottoman Empire had been under British mandate, was to be divided in 1947 into two states according to a UN resolution. The Arab-Palestinians rejected this solution (a point that is raised by Ruppin's character in the film) for violating the sovereignty and self-determination of the non-Jewish population of Palestine. This resulted in a war between the Jewish- and Arab-Palestinians and in Israel's declaration of independence. In Gal's film, the Nakba as an Arab trauma[45] is re-enacted as an expulsion from the "White City". Although Ruppin had died long before the years of the Nakba, his ideas, figures, measurements, distinction between people and ethnicities continued to spread ominously. In *White City*, events that are clearly separate in the actual order of history and/or architectural history intersect and commingle: Modernist architecture, the racist doctrine of National Socialism, Zionism, exile, the Nakba. The first shot of the film contains these confusing memes: the defamatory postcard against the Weißenhofsiedlung already engraved the sinister side of modernity onto its historical landscape.

## DOING HISTORY: STROLLING, DREAMING AND MEMORISING

All three films in the trilogy emphasise that history and the writing of it are the result of a practice. The fact that Gal's actors are exclusively male critically reflects the hegemony of the tradition of male voices and the dominance of male historiographers.[46] In Gal's films the protagonists carry out actions — sometimes in silence, since they are bound to secrecy. Actions lead to events that are memorised in turn by speaking, writing or drawing. History is narrated through the conversation between protagonists or formulated during long walks. These walks are rendered in long and slow tracking shots. They come to possess a somnambulistic power that goes hand in hand with imagination and hallucination. The theme

---

44  Bein, "Nachwort: Arthur Ruppin, der Mensch und sein Werk", p. 581.
45  On the Nakba, see Katharina Kretzschmar, *Identitäten im Konflikt: Palästinensische Erinnerung an die Nakba 1948 und deren Wirkung auf die dritte Generation*, Transcript, Bielefeld, 2019; Marlène Schnieper, *Nakba – die offene Wunde: Die Vertreibung der Palästinenser 1948 und die Folgen*, Rotpunktverlag, Zurich, 2012.
46  On this topic see Brigitte Mazohl-Wallnig, "Männer Macht Geschichte", *L'Homme: Zeitschrift für feministische Geschichtswissenschaft* 7, 1996, p. 6–33.

of walking or wandering keeps reappearing in modulations through-out the trilogy: the protagonists move with a fixed purpose or wander aimlessly through the picture. Their histories, too, are full of relocation, border crossings, escape and dispersion. Eichmann, who fled from Germany to Argentina and there — like many other National Socialist perpetrators — went into hiding, was captured by the Mossad and ab-ducted to Israel.[47] Goldman-Gilad emigrated to Palestine/Israel. And the ashes of the executed Eichmann are committed to a liquid topography without boundaries. Ruppin's Zionism, too, is based on the notion of a return to a Jewish state, while Günther's biological racism basically gave rise to persecution and forced displacement practices and extermina-tion. The motif of movement can also be transferred to representations of events that wander through disparate times and places and keep chang-ing their form, always in relation to subjects who reconstruct, describe or imagine what is past.

The trilogy implicitly acknowledges that countless other versions of received knowledge could be added to the existing ones, giving new con-texts to history — overwritten in turn by additional memories and stories. At the same time these films reflect the practices of historiography, from visualisation to suppression, and point to the permeability between fact and (cinematic) fiction without relativising the significance of sources as a door to past events. Rather, Gal's *Night and Fog*, *As from Afar* and *White City* make the case for perceiving history as a place of ongoing negotia-tion, of the coexistence and parallel existence of contradictions as some-thing that is *in motion*.

---

47  The refuge of National Socialist perpetrators in Argentina, among them Adolf Eichmann, is dealt with in literary form in Olivier Guez's novel *La disparition de Josef Mengele*, Éditions Grasset, Paris, 2017.

Set photography, *White City*, 2018, photo: Dani Gal

Filmmakers, historians, thinkers, curators, and teachers — each in his own way — assume their historical responsibility toward the future as well as their loyalty and respect for the field of creation. We all need to acknowledge that our position is not that of the knowledgeable teacher but that of the civilian who must, as either creator or intermediary, justify what we awaken or what we let lie, what we set free and what we control. And in this context, the question turns itself around one more time. It is not how the cinema and television "must transmit" or "must teach" the Shoah, but rather how the ordeal of the Shoah has completely shaken up cinematic forms of cruelty and rendered crucial the position of the receiver of all that is shown. Neither demonstrations nor visual evidence, the Shoah is a call to testify in the sharing of concern, in the production of a certain vigilance. If art is invoked, it is because we believe in the poetics of responsibility, or, if you prefer, in the ethics of passion. In this light we hope to reflect together in order to grasp something we do not grasp very well yet, especially having regained the strength we all need to resist the clear and daily threat of a return to barbarism.

Marie-José Mondzain, "The Shoah as a Question of Cinema", in *Cinema and the Shoah: An Art Confronts the Tragedy of the Twentieth Century*, ed. Jean-Michel Frodon, trans. Anna Harrison and Tom Mes, State University of New York Press, Albany, 2010, p. 14–15.

Tragically, on the practical level, recognizing the Holocaust would not have changed almost anything regarding the colonization of Palestine by the Zionist movement. This process began long before the Holocaust took place. The Palestinian experience with Jewish nationalism was fully crystalized when the latter was tightly interconnected with the British colonial endeavour to establish a Jewish state in Palestine. The Palestinian Nakba started long before 1948. For the Palestinians, Jews were not the survivors of the Holocaust, but rather those threatening their home. For Palestinians living in the 1940s, Holocaust survivors are yet *additional* Jews, who joined the movement to occupy their homeland. The challenge Palestinians faced is that the horrors of the Holocaust have been morally and practically tied with recognizing the Jewish need for a safe haven in Palestine. This linkage equated the recognition of the Holocaust with the Jewish right over the Palestinian homeland. [...] As a result, Palestinians not only agonize over the loss of their homes, but also their humanity, for not being able to fully express empathy with the ultimate victims, who then and now, are their oppressors. This tragic disposition is deepened further, as the cynical political manipulation of the Holocaust to silence the Palestinians and indirectly blame them for it increased.

Amal Jamal, "The Creative Imagination of Juxtaposing National Traumas: The Holocaust and the Nakba", *Journal of Genocide Research* 22, no. 1, 2020, p. 166–72, here p. 167–68.

# WHITE CITY: SPECTRE OF THE PALESTINIANS
## Sa'ed Atshan

May 2020. This is the month in which I watched *White City* for the first time. I was transfixed by the powerful images and dialogues on screen while simultaneously envisioning the filmmaker — the *person* behind the film — who brought these visual public commentaries to life. My cognisance of Dani Gal's positionality, namely his status as a prominent progressive Jewish-Israeli artist who has lived in Germany for many years, helps me gain a deeper appreciation for the rich conceptual horizons that undergird his prolific work. My ability to imagine him bringing his films to fruition was aided by the fact that we met two years ago during my fieldwork in Berlin. My research partner, Katharina Galor, a German-Israeli professor of Judaic Studies, and I conducted in-depth interviews for our own book project, including with Gal. The anthropological study that we completed as a result is focused on Israeli and Palestinian diaspora communities in contemporary Germany, and what we call the "moral triangle" that connects Germans, Israelis and Palestinians, historically and in the present.[1] The publication of this book coincided with my viewing of *White City*. Though we come from different backgrounds, my positionality as a progressive is, in many ways, aligned with the values and worldviews that are so dear to Gal. I confront the issues that are at the heart of his work not just as a scholar and anthropologist, but also as

---

1   See Sa'ed Atshan and Katharina Galor, *The Moral Triangle: Germans, Israelis, Palestinians*, Duke University Press, Durham, 2020.

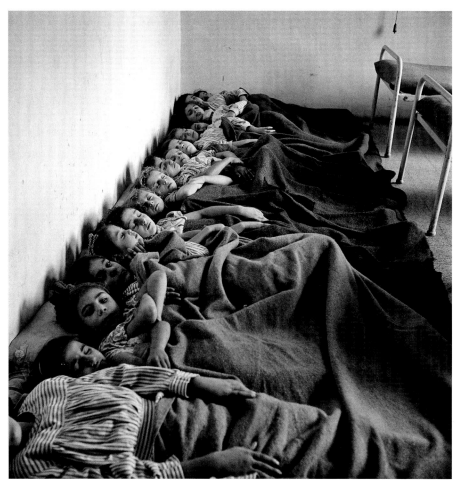

Palestinian refugee children in a Christian orphanage in Beirut, Lebanon, circa 1948–49

a Palestinian. I grew up in Palestine and cannot help but see the world through that lens, especially in domains where there is much at stake for my family, community and people. In this essay, I explore how the experience of absorbing *White City* from my vantage point is not one of alienation or marginalisation. Rather, Gal's approach to representation is affirming for a Palestinian audience, advancing an aesthetics and politics of recognition and even transcendental solidarity.

May is necessarily a tense month in Israel/Palestine. While tension is always omnipresent in the region, it has a rhythm with ebbs and flows, but May brims with pangs of desire and pain, euphoria and anguish. The contradictions that this month reveals are not tenable long term for anyone in the country. There is no movement forward toward restorative justice without a reckoning with the weight of the past. By the time May arrives, most Israelis will have just celebrated what they refer to as Yom Ha'atzmaut in Hebrew (Israel's Independence Day). They bask in the joy of the establishment of the State of Israel, what many see as a kind of miracle in the aftermath of the Holocaust. On the streets of Jerusalem, thousands and thousands of Israelis gather, marching, waving Israeli flags, chanting religious prayers out loud, singing, cheering and dancing, embracing the landing of their feet on this ancient holy land. Meanwhile, native Palestinians line up on the sidelines, behind Israeli police-enforced barricades, watching these street processions with utter helplessness, wiping tears off of their faces, calling on God to hear their prayers for justice in their ancestral homeland, holding onto loved ones for a shoulder to lean on and engaging in counter-chants if they can muster their voices and energy. Merely a few weeks later, most Palestinians are steeped in a mourning period of what they refer to as the Nakba in Arabic ("the catastrophe"), marking the destruction of Palestine and the displacement and dispossession of the Palestinian people. The commemoration by Palestinians of the Nakba as a profound historical injustice of Israel replacing Palestine is besieged by the fact that this is an ongoing process. In *White City*, Gal meets the Palestinian cry not with deaf ears; he hears our voices, deeply. Even though the Nakba has not yet occurred when the film takes place, it is always present for Gal, even when seemingly absent. As with the ghosts that haunt society and entire nations, we cannot always see what nonetheless clearly surrounds us. In this case, it is the spectre of the Palestinian subject that we cannot escape.

May of this year is also when I discovered a photograph that will haunt me forever. The Palestine Museum US in Connecticut published photographs of the Nakba from the United Nation's archive for the first time. One was a 1949 image of Palestinian girls who had lost their parents or were separated from them during the creation of Israel in 1948. The children are attempting to sleep in an orphanage in Lebanon, crowded together on the floor with uncomfortable pillows and blankets, in striped uniforms and looks of bewilderment on their faces. The oppression and despair that life has thrown their way is palpable; they have no space to properly breathe. I could not peel my eyes from the photograph. I learned from friends that Palestinians in the diaspora were literally putting pieces of the puzzle together to determine whether the image of one of these girls was in fact their own grandmother. Sometimes the pain is difficult to bear because we know that as Palestinians our humanity is called into question. What provides me with solace is that our families and communities continue to forge networks and ties of love and a cognisance that injustice cannot last forever. The Nakba is not over. But what gets lost in the political debates and in the discourse of Palestinian intellectuals like Edward Said — who once wrote that "we are the victims of the victims, the refugees of the refugees"[2] — are the human faces and stories that underlie this victimhood. Without existing knowledge of the context, many individuals would assume that this black-and-white image is of Jewish girls in a Nazi concentration camp. And even with the knowledge that they are indeed Palestinian girls in a Lebanese orphanage, the weight of the Holocaust is present in that room. The liberation of the Nazi camps was soon followed by the establishment of this orphanage. One tragedy succeeds the other and the two will forever be inextricably intertwined. Naming this reality is a tremendously fraught exercise: politically, intellectually and spiritually. As Galor and I explicate in our book, the Holocaust and the Nakba are not identical historical events but they are fundamentally linked. The Israeli state derives formidable moral legitimacy because of the former, and Germany justifies its support for the Israeli state also because of the former. Yet the latter, the Nakba, is elided — the Palestinian voice and body are often erased from collective consciousness. As a result, I argue that ghosts of the Nakba haunt artistic representations of the Holocaust today, and ghosts of the Holocaust haunt representations of the Nakba today. While seeing this particular photograph at the same time as *White City*, I registered how these two forces, of the Holocaust on one hand and the Nakba on the other, come together very poignantly in Gal's work.

This connection is revealed in the scene between Hans F. K. Günther, one of the leading proponents of Nazi racial theory, and Arthur Ruppin, a Jewish Zionist from Germany who was one of the founders of Tel Aviv and engineered the first settlement group relocation and facilitation of Zionist migration to Palestine. In the script, the question arises of whether Günther views Ruppin as inferior because of his Jewish

---

2    Edward Said, "The One-State Solution", *New York Times Magazine*, 10 January, 1999, section 6, p. 36.

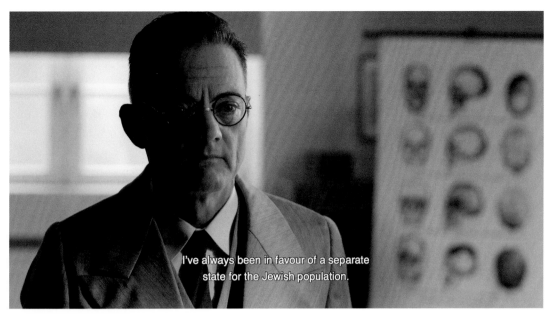

I've always been in favour of a separate
state for the Jewish population.

I follow the Zionist ambitions with interest.

Dani Gal, *White City*, 2018, film stills, camera: Itay Marom

rundown Arab villages,

Dani Gal, *White City*, 2018, film still, camera: Itay Marom

Hans Thoma, *Der Wanderer*, lithograph, 1906

Portrait of Arthur Ruppin
by L. Danziger, April 1900

background. Günther denies this, arguing instead that he believes in the separation between Nordic and Semitic peoples. He expresses support for the Zionist movement's settlements in Palestine precisely in order to uproot Jewish populations from Europe. Ruppin seems unfazed by the fact that Günther supports his political project, instead mirroring this desire to segregate and dominate. These realities are deeply uncomfortable and rarely acknowledged in German mainstream public discourse today, given the country's disavowal of the Holocaust and efforts to atone for these crimes. Countless Germans identify with the Israeli state as a way to compensate for the sins of anti-Semitism and the Holocaust. However, Israel is conveniently located in a distant land. It is striking in *White City* that Germans like Günther found it completely normal to utter the word "Palestine" in the run-up to Israel's creation, when it is a challenging word to utter for so many Germans and Israelis today. Gal compels his audience to reckon with a prominently displayed map of Palestine for much of the film. It is unnerving to sense the parallels in Günther and Ruppin's discourses and ideologies of naturalising hierarchies, engineering the "weeding out" of those who are rendered inferior, ascribing intellectual and physical traits to those who are rendered superior.

Over the course of *White City*, there are German-Zionist refrains of a shared architecture between Germany and the Zionist project in Palestine: desiring shared forests and landscapes between the countries, desiring the proliferation of affective ties across these boundaries. Gal's representation of the German-Zionist aesthetics and ideology is not meant to euphemise; rather, he signals its deeply disturbing features. This is elicited through evocative images such as literal measurements of noses, charts of human skulls, a collection of eyeballs and most disconcertingly, the description of Palestinians as residing in "barren" lands and "rundown Arab villages". I could not help but think of my grandmother throughout the film and the genuine question she often posed as a survivor of the Nakba as to why the international community and Zionist movement did not create Israel in Germany instead of Palestine. Of course, she recognised that there were Jewish populations for whom Israel/Palestine was indeed the land of their forefathers, that Jewish refugees were escaping anti-Semitism, persecution and genocide and that Palestine was better off as a pluralistic place that embraced Jews, Christians and Muslims equally. Nonetheless, she struggled to understand how the world's conscience would permit one profound injustice in the name of remedying another.

The banality of evil: A truck arrives in front of the Weißenhofsiedlung and Palestinians gather to load their belongings and themselves on it; a juxtaposition of the Israeli ethnic-cleansing process and the modernist ideals of 1927 architecture erected in Stuttgart. Gal's film trilogy starts with the quintessential example of the banality of evil with the depiction of the immediate aftermath of Adolf Eichmann's trial in Jerusalem. The trilogy ends with the victims becoming perpetrators as soon as they attain the machinery and power of a nation state. This end shot coincides with the positioning of the camel, coming full circle from the film's opening shot of a Nazi "propaganda" postcard forewarning of an Arab takeover of the newly built Weißenhofsiedlung. The closing scene is the actualisation of that very black-and-white photomontage, which also bears resemblance to the rapid development of Tel Aviv during that time. The camel becomes a symbol of Zionist colonialism and the Nakba it caused. Through positioning the two Bedouin men next to the camel, they become historical witnesses to the tragedy as opposed to the truck driver who simply looks away. Most Palestinians at the time led largely agricultural lives, but they come across on screen as primitive with an emphasis on the Bedouin population: shapeless, nameless and faceless. Urban, cosmopolitan Palestinian women and men from cities such as Jerusalem, Jaffa and Haifa experienced their Nakba exile differently from the downtrodden shipped on trucks. I could not envision my grandmother among the Palestinian Arab women who appear at the film's closing.

The film reveals a masculinist harshness to the German-Zionist nexus, with a saturated focus on forceful male bodies and voices. I held on to the tenderness of the performance of Yousef Sweid in the film and the gentle masculinity that he embodied. This famous Palestinian-Israeli actor is cast as a German Jew, and the character expresses clear ambivalence — or even suspicion — towards the Zionist narratives demanding European settlement in Palestine. The appearance of Sweid in this manner was a subversive act on the part of the filmmaker, highlighting that Jewish, Arab and European populations are all internally heterogeneous and that Zionism has had its thoughtful critics from each of these communities in the past and in the present. This is another form of Gal's affirmation of Palestinian humanity in the face of European and Israeli colonial denial and erasure. Gal is not unique in his insistence on the central role of Palestinian suffering as part of the explication of German-Israeli history. Yet, we must identify the need for cinematic expression and cultural critique on a set of issues such as this one, anaemic in its representation if left only to the musings of intellectuals and politicians.

In *Night and Fog*'s closing scene, the police boat crosses a fishing boat from Jaffa early in the morning. In their original interview, Michael Goldman-Gilad told Gal that when the officers came back to shore after scattering Eichmann's ashes, they saw fishermen from Jaffa going out to sea. This gave Gal the idea to create an exchange of gazes between the Israeli policemen and the Palestinian fisherman in the context of Eichmann's execution: a poignant manifestation of the German-Israeli-Palestinian

Set photography, *White City*, 2018, photo: Klaus Oppermann

Palestinian refugees fleeing their villages during the Nakba, 1948

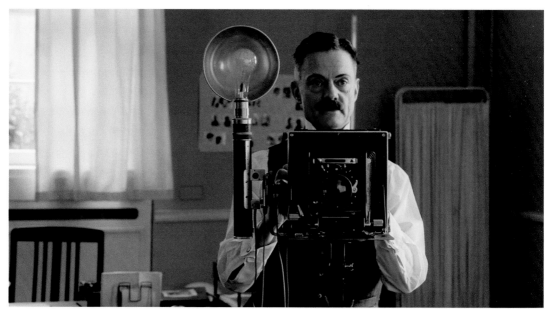

Dani Gal, *White City*, 2018, film stills, camera: Itay Marom

moral triangle. Gal felt that this gaze was best expressed by the Israeli poet Avoth Yeshurun, who understood the Nakba early on.

While it is difficult to translate from Hebrew, the poet's chosen name of Avoth Yeshurun means something along the lines of "Fathers looked straight in the eyes". Yeshurun articulated the emotional intensity of his memories of landing in Haifa from Poland and when a Palestinian sailor had taken him off the ship when he arrived. Yeshurun identified his father as being constituted in two parts: his biological father who enabled him to leave Poland and the Palestinian sailor who first carried his hand as an arriving immigrant. In the scene at sea, Gal captures the mutual suspicion between the Israeli policemen and the Palestinian fishermen, but there is simultaneously also a moment of mutual recognition with Gal's recreation of Yeshurun's gaze. Yeshurun was haunted by the spectre of the Palestinian subject, and Gal is haunted by that haunting. In absorbing Gal's work, we become part of this collective gaze, bearing witness to the Palestinian cry for freedom.

Dani Gal, *Night and Fog*, 2011, film still, camera: Itay Marom

I requested permission from my father to take leave,
which he gave and took his leave. An Arab sailor in Haifa
lifted me up onto the land and it allowed him to take
his leave.

The Holocaust of the Jews of Europe and the Holocaust
of the Arabs of Erets Yisrael are one Holocaust of the
Jewish people. The two gaze directly into one another's
face.

It is of this that I speak.

1958.

Avot Yeshurun, *Kol shirav*, vol. 1, p. 104, trans. Lisa Katz, in Hannan Hever, *Hebrew Literature and the 1948 War: Essays on Philology and Responsibility*, Brill, Leiden, 2019, p. 77.

# SOURCES

All film stills from the trilogy are courtesy of the artist and Kadel Willborn, Düsseldorf.

| | |
|---|---|
| 10 | English translation courtesy of Sharon Krebs |
| 25 | Courtesy Simon Wiesenthal Archive, Vienna Wiesenthal Institute |
| 29 | Courtesy Israel Government Press Office (D409-040) |
| 41 | Courtesy Kibbutz Gaash (CC BY 2.0) |
| 42 | Courtesy Haaretz |
| 48 | Two bottom images: Courtesy Argos Films |
| 54 | Courtesy Simon Wiesenthal Archive, Vienna Wiesenthal Institute |
| 56 | Courtesy Liliana Cavani |
| 60 | © Framepool (521-920-893) |
| 61 | Courtesy Schwäbischer Heimatbund |
| 62 | © Alamy Stock Photo (MY84W6) |
| 66 | Courtesy of Peter Gessner and United States Holocaust Memorial Museum (81197) |
| 75 | Courtesy Mercedes-Benz Classic (6075) |
| 85 | Left bottom: Courtesy Yad Vashem (1572/80) |
| | Right bottom: Courtesy Yad Vashem (3154/2) |
| 86 | Courtesy Yad Vashem (1605/17) |
| 92 | Courtesy Bundesdenkmalamt, Federal Monuments Authority Austria |
| 97 | Top: Courtesy Stadtarchiv Stuttgart (9450_A374_c_01) |
| | Bottom: Courtesy Manfred Ulmer |
| 101 | Left bottom: Courtesy Central Zionist Archives |
| | Right bottom: © Bundesarchiv (Bild 183-1989-0912-500) |
| 112 | Courtesy United Nations (UN7720762) |
| 116 | Left bottom: Courtesy Lauinger Verlag Karlsruhe |
| | Right bottom: Courtesy Central Zionist Archives |
| 119 | Middle: © CPA Media Pte Ltd / Alamy Stock Photo (2B0302K) |
| | Bottom: Courtesy Israel Government Press Office (D275-120) |

# WORK LIST

An Elaborate Gesture of Pastness

*Night and Fog*, 2011
Duration: 22 minutes
Featuring Yaron Mottola, Moris Cohen and John Fulton
Written and directed by Dani Gal
Produced by Jonathan Dowek and Dani Gal
Premiered at the 54th Venice Biennale, 2011

*As from Afar*, 2013
Duration: 26 minutes
Featuring Pavel Fieber, Charles Brauer and Gideon Singer
Directed by Dani Gal
Written by Sascha Reh and Dani Gal
Produced by Caroline Kirberg and Dani Gal
Premiered at Kunst Halle Sankt Gallen, 2013

*White City*, 2018
Duration: 25 minutes
Featuring Alexander E. Fennon, Christian Harting and Yousef Sweid
Directed by Dani Gal
Written by Esther Kinsky and Dani Gal
Produced by Pong Film, Caroline Kirberg and Dani Gal
Premiered at Staatsgalerie Stuttgart, 2019

# BIOGRAPHIES

SA'ED ATSHAN is associate professor of Peace and Conflict Studies at Swarthmore College, where he is also coordinator of the Mellon Mays Undergraduate Fellowship Program. As an anthropologist and peace and conflict studies scholar, Atshan's research is focused on contemporary Palestinian society and politics, global LGBTQ+ social movements, and Quaker Studies and Christian minorities in the Middle East. He is the author of *Queer Palestine and the Empire of Critique* (Stanford University Press, 2020), and co-author with Katharina Galor of *The Moral Triangle: Germans, Israelis, Palestinians* (Duke University Press, 2020).

NOIT BANAI is an art historian and critic who has taught internationally at NYU Shanghai, University of Vienna and Tufts University /School of the Museum of Fine Arts, Boston. Her monograph *Yves Klein* appeared in Reaktion's Critical Lives series in 2014, and she is currently completing a book titled *Between Nation State and Border State: Modernism from Universal to Global Subject*, which examines particular artistic strategies and structures that have complicated the universal model of the European public sphere from 1938 to the present.

SABETH BUCHMANN is an art historian and art critic. She is professor of Modern and Postmodern Art at the Vienna Academy of Fine Arts. Buchmann researches conceptual forms of work in the visual arts, respectively in performance, film and new media. Her current teaching and upcoming book and exhibition projects will cover topoi and procedures of (un-)learning and rehearsal as part of the infrastructural analysis of modern and contemporary art and art education. She is the author of *Denken gegen das Denken: Produktion Technologie Subjektivität bei Sol LeWitt, Yvonne Rainer and Hélio Oiticica* (b_books, 2007). As co-editor, publications include: *Putting Rehearsals to the Test: Practices of Rehearsal in Fine Arts, Film, Theater, Theory, and Politics* (Sternberg Press, 2016), *Hélio Oiticica and Neville D'Almeida: Block-Experiments in Cosmococa—program in progress* (Afterall, 2013), *Film, Avantgarde, Biopolitik* (Schlebrügge.Editor, 2009) and *Art After Conceptual Art* (MIT Press, 2006). Buchmann is currently co-editor of PoLYpeN, a book series on art criticism and political theory published by b_books, Berlin, and a member of the advisory board of *Texte zur Kunst*, the Escola das Artes – Universidade Católica Portuguesa and the Austrian Ludwig Foundation Board of Trustees.

BURCU DOGRAMACI is a professor at the Institute for Art History at the Ludwig Maximilian University of Munich with a focus on twentieth-century and contemporary art. Her research on exile, migration and flight in the past and present is dedicated to forms of migration / migration of forms, the concepts and aesthetics of an art production of exile, non-linear and anachronistic historiographies, transcultural networks, as well as the theories and methods of an art history in motion. Publications include *Arrival Cities: Migrating Artists and New Metropolitan Topographies in the 20th Century* (Leuven University Press, 2020) and *Fotografie der Performance: Live Art im Zeitalter ihrer Reproduzierbarkeit* (Fink, 2018).

# COLOPHON

AN ELABORATE GESTURE
OF PASTNESS
Three Films by Dani Gal

Editors
Dani Gal
Mika Hayashi Ebbesen

Authors
Sa'ed Atshan
Noit Banai
Sabeth Buchmann
Burcu Dogramaci
Dani Gal

Translation
Ilze Mueller (Dogramaci)

Copy editing
Mika Hayashi Ebbesen

Proofreading
Mark Soo

Graphic design
Olga Prader

Cover
Dani Gal

Produced by
Blood Mountain Projects

Published by
Motto Books, Berlin/Lausanne

Printed by
SYL, Barcelona

Distributed by
Motto Distribution

ISBN: 978-2-940672-21-9

© 2021 Motto Books, Dani Gal,
Blood Mountain Projects
and the authors

This publication has been made possible by the generous support of the Bundeskanzleramt –
Federal Chancellery Republic of Austria, the Ernst & Olga Gubler-Hablützel Foundation, the Nationalfonds
– National Fund of the Republic of Austria for Victims of National Socialism and the Zukunftsfonds –
Future Fund of the Republic of Austria.

# ACKNOWLEDGEMENTS

Special thanks goes to Peter Banki, Nadia Guth Biasini, René Bienert, Etan Blum, Shannon Bool, Giovanni Carmine, Liliana Cavani, Jean-Claude Freymond-Guth, Adi Gal, Avi and Bori Gal, Echo Gal, Péter Garai, Amos Goldberg, Michael Goldman-Gilad, Assaf Gruber, Emma Waltraud Howes, Eva Kovacs, the Migros Museum für Gegenwartskunst, Jade Niklai, Amir Peleg, Karin Pernegger, Béla Rásky, Nadia Schneider Willen, Tom Segev, Tom Sloan, Manfred Ulmer, the Vienna Wiesenthal Institute and Amon Yariv.